THE FORGOTTEN PEOPLES

IRONS, WHIPS, CHAINS AND SHACKLES

The Slavery and Plight of the Roma Gypsies

By

RAY WILLS

(THE GYPSY POET)

Copyright © 2023 Ray Wills

A GYPSY POET PUBLICATION

Cover image courtesy of Dawn Jeanette Grant Harrison

ISBN: 9798388783226

One day the white men arrived in ships with wings, which shone in the sun like knives, They fought hard battles with the Ngola and spat fire at him. They conquered his salt pans and the Ngola fled inland to the Lukala River....

Pende oral tradition.

CONTENTS

ILLUSTRATIONS AND PICTURES

GYPSY SLAVES
Art Picture Courtesy of Dawn Jeanette Grant Harrison

DOCKSIDE SLAVE TRADE

WOOL BRIDGE MANOR HOUSE
Drax family

WOOL BRIDGE TRANSPORTATION NOTICE
On the bridges

DRAX HALL BARBADOS
Charborough house 1774

PRESS GANGS

PORTLAND PRESS GANGS NOTICE

WHITE SLAVERY IN THE EAST
Christian prisoners Algiers

HOLOCAUST
Courtesy of Dawn Jeanette Grant Harrison

ACKNOWLEDGEMENTS

The Author wishes to acknowledge with many thanks the Artist Dawn Jeannette Grant Harrison contribution of her art work for the book's front cover.

ABOUT THE AUTHOR

Ray Wills was born in Newtown Poole Dorset in 1945. Rays childhood and early youth was spent in Dorset on the Mannings heathland Poole Next door to the Dorset councils Gypsy traveller encampment.

Then later he lived at Wareham before returning to Parkstone and attending Kemp Welch school. After leaving school his first job was as a painter and chassis sprayer for Bluebird Caravans the largest caravan industry in the world. Than he was an Officers Batman in Bovington Camp Dorset before joining Community Service Volunteers.

It was whilst he was on a CSV project that Ray first worked closely with the National Playing Fields Association. Then for many decades afterwards he was involved in the establishment and management of numerous children's adventure playgrounds and play projects throughout the UK in inner cities and rural communities.

Ray has been a member of numerous poetry groups in Dorset a member of Kushti Bok the Gypsy Roma Traveller organisation and is a social historian and an authority on the history of the Gypsy community. His qualifications include a Royal Society of Arts Diploma in Management and Senior Youth worker City and Guilds certificate. At present he lives within a community of artists, writers and musicians in the village of Bere Regis in Dorset. Here he continues to give talks on local history and poetry readings throughout Dorset. Ray is project co ordinator and historian of Kushti Bok the Gypsy traveller welfare organisation. He works closely with both Poole and Dorchester Museums and the Dorchester Heritage centre. He operates numerous community organisation pages on Facebook.

Ray Wills previous publications have included, "The Gypsy Storyteller" anthology, for Francis Boutle Publisher, "Romance in the Everglades" poetry anthology- published by xpress publications. "The Canford Chronicles -A poetry Anthology, "Where the River Bends", "Adventures in Child's Play". "The Gypsy Camp", "The Time Traveller","Starlight Afore the Dew"- A poetry anthology and "Gypsy Tales". He regularly writes numerous articles for magazines including the "Traveller Times" and "Play and Playground".

INTRODUCTION

"Where was I now?. I looked around the place it looked like the quay, but was very different. The houses were shacks here now, situated amongst the great elegant Georgian pillared homes. The Inns were still here and I recognised the *Ship inn, the Jolly Sailor* and another which looked like *the Lord Nelson*. There were stone slabbing foundations pavements and stone bollards and large stone blocks. It was thronged with people here with large ships Galleon's in the harbour. Plus heavy horse driven wagons on the quayside all loaded up with nigh 2 hundred weight large sacks of animal feeds, corn and molasses. There was a strong smell of salt and fish in the air.Towards the left of the quay were many stalls and here there was a large crowd of Gypsy women. They were with each holding long knives stripping and gutting cod fish, salting them and putting them into heavy clay jugs. There were a vast variety of newly caught fish here. Mostly cod from the New Found Land trade. I saw winkles and mussels too. There were large warehouses which I recognised and knew were to become storage for the nearby warehouses of the animal foods company and others. Nearby stood the town hall proud and majestically with its stoned steps and back iron hand railing. Amongst the crowds were sailors easily recognised by their caps and their colourful cotton scarves around their heads and around their necks. All of them busily, working, loading and unloading from the many many ships and boats in the harbour.

I watched as young men lined up to sign up for apprentice ships and as indentured volunteers. Destined to sail on the next boats to work at the new world cotton, tobacco and sugar plantations and particularly on the New Found Land ships. The light blue sky was full of noisy squawking sea gulls. I saw a large crowd gathered towards the front of the harbour. These I recognised as men of the cloth amongst them, those of the church cardinals and others in their black and red clothing. Along with the wealthy looking local gentlemen merchants and traders wearing their fine Georgian hats, long coats, fancy waistcoats and buckled shoes. I stepped a little closer to the gathering it looked like they were auctioning something.As I stepped closer I saw the large stone blocks. I recognised them from the history books as auction blocks. There stood a tall handsome dark African man with a tall black top hat perched elegantly on his head he was obviously the auctioneer. Standing on the blocks were a small number of black and white young men and women. The men were bare chested with short trousers and shoes whilst the women wore long skimpy simple dresses which showed off their fine young figures. All of them were shackled on their legs with iron ball and chains and some had deep cuts marking on their bodies. Then I heard the loud voice of the young auctioneer booming out amongst the crowds. He said "come gentlemen here's a bargain, a fine young darky stud from the continent, he is strong and masculine with good teeth and the strength of a lion". "Who will offer me a fair price?." Then I heard the taller of the merchant gentleman speak. He said "I offer 10 pounds, for there's no fortune in this young rascal he could be more bother than time warrants." The young auctioneer responded to his response, "Well then gentleman any offers on this here young beautiful Gypsy girl. She's just sixteen a virgin beauty with fine figure lovely ripe tits and beautiful firm ass cheeks. She will excel in your bed and satisfy your every need." He said "She will wait on you hand and foot" "Any offers".There was lots of talk amongst the distinguished looking gentlemen present there and as the auction went on with much interest amongst them particularly in the young Gypsy girl. Then the auctioneer said "Gentleman I have an offer of 20 pounds, a small fortune for this girl"."She comes with a pedigree, for her family are well respected local forest people". "She can cook for you, she will make your bed and lay in it for your pleasure.".".She can sing, as she has a beautiful voice to send you to sleep with her lullaby's." He said "Any more offers gentlemen."

The same distinguished looking gentleman spoke again "I offer 30 pounds and that's my limit" said the fine looking man who I noticed wore a royal crest on his arm.

He then raised his voice again and said" I am from the Queens counsel I am lord of this manor and I need a good wench, my offer goes without warrant". Then the auctioneer shouted "Sold to the fine gentleman."

The man made his way to the blocks and the auctioneer unlocked the girls ankle chains with his key and set her free. The gentleman gave the auctioneer a small bundle of large notes out of his thick fine leather wallet and he swiftly disappeared with the girl into the crowd with the girl holding onto his hand tightly.

I reflected on the fact that the term Gentlemen here was closely associated with the Newfound trade from Poole and the colony planters. Its rich merchants were no doubt an essential part of this slave trading. For as Daniel Defoe noted "trade, in England, makes gentlemen" and involvement in the Newfoundland trade was a way of becoming rich and attaining social status.

The crowds here were immense now, there was lots of pushing and shoving and the noise of the busy ships and sailors made it even more deafening. Then I heard the auctioneer shout out. "That's all for today gentlemen, same time the morrow with new slaves for the plantations." he said "Good day gentlemen."

Extract from my book The Time Traveller.
Available from Amazon.

"Gypsies shall be born only slaves; anyone born of a slave mother shall also become a slave…" stated the code of Wallachia at the beginning of the 19th century.

The term slave has its origins in the word slav. The slavs were a people who inhabited a large part of Eastern Europe of slave people. They were taken as slaves by the Muslims of Spain during the 9th century. In 1172 in Ireland the clergy began to reproach themselves because they had bought as slaves the English boys brought to them by the merchants. In the 13th century the custom prevailed on the continent of Europe to treat all captives taken in war, as slaves. From the early 13th to the mid 15th century, Italian merchants transported tens of thousands of Slav people as slaves, of whom a good proportion were used for the production of sugar. But the capture of Constantinople in 1453 stopped this flow causing the Italian merchants to look westwards for a new source of supply. In Europe it was held lawful to enslave any infidel or person who did not receive the Christian faith.

By the middle of the 19th century there were half a million slaves on Romanian territory. Unfortunately, until now, Gypsy Roma slavery has not yet been included in most history school books, and there are still very few who are aware of this historical reality. As a general rule the word Slavery itself refers to a condition in which one human being is owned by another. Slavery can best be described as the ownership, buying and selling of human beings for the purpose of forced and unpaid labour.

Slavery may well exist without torture, for slaves may in fact still be well fed, clothed and cared for. But they still are slaves if denied their freedom. Although there is no such thing as benevolent slavery. For involuntary servitude still remains as slavery. The practice of Slavery was conducted at one time by all nations throughout history. Not only were there black slaves as we are aware and were taught. But also there were white slaves these were slaves of all nations and races including Gypsies.

Muslim nations and Christian nations alike all were at some point in history involved in the trafficking of slaves.

Slaves were used as labour for work on the plantations in the mines and in the monasteries as well as on the battlefields throughout history. People were taken as prisoner slaves by conquering armies, pirates or even by their own rulers, to man their warships and to work in their ship galleys or to be sold for work on the New World cotton, tobacco and sugar plantations. In the America and the Caribbean. Slavery has existed practically upon nearly every continent, including Asia, Europe, Africa, and the Americas, and throughout most of recorded history. It dwelled in every nation of the world. It was accepted by the ancient Greeks and Romans who accepted its institution. As did others such as the Mayas, Incas, Aztecs, and Chinese. Varro, a Roman philosopher stated in his agricultural manuscripts that white slaves were only things with a voice or instrumenti vocali. Julius Caesar enslaved as many as one million whites from Gaul. Slavery appears in the tents of Abraham, for the 318 servants born to him were slaves. It appears in the story of Joseph, who was sold by his brothers to the Midinettes for twenty pieces of silver. It appears in the poetry of Homer, who stamps it with a reprobation which can never be forgotten, when he says

Jove fixed it certain, that whatever day
Makes man a slave takes half his worth away

In Greece the great philosopher Plato in his imaginary Republic sanctioned slavery. Whilst Paulus Emilas returned from Macedni with an uncounted train of slaves, composed of persons in every department of life. At the Romen camp of Lucilius, in Pontius, slaves were sold for four dracmas, Or seventy two cents a head.From Antiquity, European slaves were common during the reign of Ancient Rome and were prominent during the Ottoman Empire. They could be bought and sold as property and were subject to labour and branding by their owners. Under Muslim rule, the Arab slave trade that included Caucasian captives were often fuelled by raids into European territories. Or were taken as children in the form of a blood tax from the families of citizens of conquests, to serve the empire for a variety of functions. The Scots survived slavery for a thousand years. According to these resources as well as many more, the Scots-Irish have been enslaved longer than any other race in the world's history. The early ancestors of the Scots, Alba and Pics were enslaved as early as the first century BC.Yet despite this when one thinks of slavery one might think of Africans picking cotton in the fields of America. Books such as "Uncle Toms Cabin", the TV series Roots or the Rev Martin Luther King speech I have a dream and the race protest marches with Dylan. Many still do not know that it was the Irish who preceded the Africans as slaves in the early British colonies of America and the West Indies.

Its involvement in Europe in the 16th century, was a more public and "racially" based style of slavery. When we are told that Europeans began importing slaves from Africa to the New World. With some 11 million estimated people being taken from Africa in what became known as the transatlantic slave trade. When more than four million were imported to the America. Despite slave imports being banned from 1809.The majority of the Africans who were sent to the United States to work on the cotton or rice plantations in the South. Approaching half of them were transported from Africa to the Americas were taken to Brazil where they worked in harsh conditions. Whilst England had similar sugar colonies in the Caribbean at West Indies Isles of Barbados and

Jamaica.The slave trade however was responsible for bringing many to England in the 17ᵗʰ and 18ᵗʰ centuries. As well as changing the ethnic make up of the country. This trade in human beings brought in huge wealth to Britain and the financial effects of slavery are still with us today. Along with many areas of our thinking which had their origins in colonial times.In my search through research for this present work I was greatly impressed by the great deal of historical research which previously had been undertaken and successfully achieved on the subject of White slavery. By imminent historians and writers of our present decade, whom I read thoroughly and I acknowledge and have quote throughout this present work. Notably these are Robert Dawson, Professor Robert Davis, Ian Hancock and Matthew Parker,After the rise of abolitionism, Britain outlawed slavery in its colonies in 1833, and France did the same in 1848. Despite this, slavery continues to exist in many parts of the world. Many contemporary slaves are women and children forced into prostitution or working at hard labour or in sweatshops. Debt bondage is common, affecting millions of people, and slaves are often traded for material goods.Following the most recent Black Lives Matter protests, the bend of knees movement.

The Oliver Cromwellian regime was the first English government to dedicate itself to building a plantation empire based on the permanent enslavement of Africans. The form of chattel labour that would dominate the Atlantic world for the next two centuries. Race matters in the history of slavery and in the Janus-faced struggles for justice in our own time. In this light, the history of Irish slavery should lead to solidarity with—rather than scorn for—the deep history driving the Black Lives Matter movement. Interracial solidarity may be the only means by which we can lift the curse of Cromwell that still haunts the Irish in America.

Yet few people are actually also aware of the long history of slavery amongst the White community, or even of those from the Gypsy community who were taken as slaves. For throughout the centuries Gypsies have been the victims of oppression and slavery by both the Muslim and the Christian nations. They had endured expulsions, the forcible removal of their children and then slavery and servitude on plantations as well as in galleys and mines. The death sentence was often dished out to many of them for nothing more than for just being a Gypsy.

The Persecution of Gypsies in particular came from and was endorsed within the highest authorities of both State and the Church over the centuries. Few groups of people have suffered more than the universal fear, loathing and banishment which has been and still is experienced by Gypsies and Travellers, known in mainland Europe as Gypsy Roma Travellers.Gypsy Roma Travellers were the forgotten people amongst the white slaves of the New World and the West Indies. Many of whom were shipped on slave ships from our British ports. They were sold as slaves on blocks. Many thousands were persecuted, transported, hung or imprisoned at the order of Kings and Queens such as James I, Henry V111,Queen Elizabeth 1 and leaders such as Oliver Cromwell and later Germany with Hitler and the Holocaust. It has been suggested by many that white slavery had been minimised or ignored because academics preferred to treat Europeans as evil colonialists rather than as victims of a white slave trade. Whilst this neglect of Roma Gypsy history is common across much of Europe and in the UK.Present day historian Robert Dawson commented, "You will find that there is no mention of Gypsy slavery in any of the official books on slavery. Yet huge numbers of Gypsies were shipped in iron chains and shackles from countries such as Spain and Portugal to their American colonies and to Africa". Whilst others were transported from London, Liverpool, Bristol and Weymouth to slave plantations in Barbados. Though there is little or no mention of Great British involvement with White people or Gypsies as slaves in any non specialist text.Gypsies were just seen as British subjects who had chosen to abandoned their rights to freedom and were no more than just criminals, misfits or vagrants. Some of these also may well have travelled elsewhere were sold as slaves in Constantinople in 1657.

In England in1660 a new company entitled "The Royal Adventurers into Africa" was established in London by Prince Rupert. This body was to gain a trade monopoly for centuries as the English trade with Africa. It included within its membership many prominent politicians, Lords, church officials and Royalty. Included amongst hundreds of its members were Barons, Dukes, Earls and Knights. It represented the most prominent members of the British establishment.

The Royal Adventurers later included members of the royal family including the king, along with Queen Catherine the daughter of the king of Portugal. At the beginning a quarter of this new African trade was devoted to slaves. In 1665 the company estimated its annual return from slaves was £100,000.

Often pirates or corsairs boarded ships and captured those on board as slaves too, some were usually resold.The forcible removal of Gypsies from our shores then shipped to the New world of the America and the Caribbean is hardly mentioned, or not at all in any of our literature. It is still very apparent that so very little is recorded in any England official documents. For none of these official books make any mention of the thousands of Gypsies who were enslaved. Yet a vast number of European people people were shipped in irons as slaves to the American colonies and to work the Caribbean islands plantations. Attacks on the slave ships by pirate ships to obtain slaves was also very common.Modern day school history classes present indentured servitude as a benignly paternalistic system whereby colonial immigrants spent a few years working off their passage and went on to better things. Not so, this impassioned history argues: For the indentured servitude of whites was comparable in most respects to the slavery endured by blacks. For voluntary indentured servants arriving in colonial America and the West Indies from Britain were sold on the blocks. In Barbados thousands were subjected to backbreaking work on the sugar plantations there, poorly fed and clothed, savagely punished for any disobedience, forbidden to marry without their master's permission, and whipped and branded for running away.

Nor were indentures always voluntary: tens of thousands of convicts, beggars, homeless children and other undesirable Britons were transported to America against their will particularly by Oliver Cromwell. Given the hideous mortality rates, the authors argue, indentured contracts often amounted to a life sentence at hard labour—some convicts asked to be hanged rather than be sent to the colonies.In recent times particularly with the broader public discourse that has emerged since the murder of George Floyd. The national curriculums of the UK have received greater scrutiny for the whitewashing of history and the narratives that are taught to students. UK children are required by law to be taught about the Holocaust in their key stage 3 education, yet there is no statutory requirement for children to be taught about Romani genocide in the Holocaust. Or the fact that a century before Britain was itself involved in the Trans-Atlantic slave trade, when whole villages and communities in England, Ireland, Scotland, Wales, Italy, Spain and other European nations were being systematically being depopulated by slavers. Slave ships also transported them all, men, women and children to Africa and the West Indies.

Many of them were Gypsies. These people were sold as slaves to the highest bidders with many of them put to work on the tobacco and sugar plantations. This is the forgotten white slave trade. Expulsions, enslavement, and discriminatory laws have plagued the Gypsies very existence for centuries throughout history.

Slavery was a very lucrative and profitable enterprising venture and many men became very rich as Slavers, merchants and plantation owners. Those involved in the slave trade became respectable gentlemen, this was particularly so in the British Isles for hundreds of years. Their family names became well known and they gained great prestige particularly from the Government and the Royalty. As a result many were knighted and then when slavery was eventually abolished in the UK they were well paid compensation fortunes for their loss of earnings by the British government. Unfortunately in the mid-19th century, the term 'white slavery' was only used to describe the Christian slaves that were sold into the terrible Barbary slave trade. In 2019, two activists took to the streets of Bucharest to interview passers-by on the topic of Roma slavery in Romania. Many of those they encountered knew nothing or little about Roma slavery. The activists drew attention to the omission of Roma slavery in the Romanian school curriculum. Historian Prof. Davis - "white slaves with non-white masters simply do no fit "the master narrative of European imperialism."

"The victimization schemes so dear to academics require white wickedness, not white suffering".

CHAPTER ONE

EARLY GYPSY SLAVES AND CONFLICTS

EXODUS

In the Indian continent where Hindi was brave
they danced and they sang like Sultans enslaved
amidst armies advancing amidst treasons and plots
they humbled themselves for all that they got

They played to the kings and fought in the wars
they were slaves to the rich
and they danced for both rich and the poor
they fled from the terrors of mans arms and wars
in the battles that raged there
and the mights of the swords

They were shackled as slaves tortured and maimed
their brethren were scattered through valleys and flames
the music they played there
when the folks all did dance
whilst all their lives were in torment
imprisoned and chanced

They fled to Europe through Egypts great plains
their tales they all told whilst they played all the games
from tyrant doctrines of torment and pain
then they gathered their brothers and rode on again

Ray Wills

The Glory Days of Babylon

The carousel bandits rode o'er the plains
they were gathered in dust with gold on their reins
their ponies were bridled and their history begins
where the trail blazing stops and the saga begins

There was blood on their hands but their spirits were blessed
they stored all their glories in their treasure chests
where the banners were flying and the anthems did play
in the mornings of battle in the first light of day

All the history books told it and the drums they did roll
where the parchments of stanzas were chiselled in snow
on the rocks of the hillsides where the coyotes ran free
where the winds they did blow in the sanctuary of free

The aged librarian wrote all the text
then kindled his memories in the words of the wretch
where the annuals of time set the anchors so deep
in the banks of the harbours where no man did sleep

Oh the bugles they sounded and the glories were cast
upon the hillsides amongst hidden paths
where the victories of battles were stolen in lies
where Truth has no Honour amongst masons and spies

Ray Wills

White slavery (also known as white slave trade or white slave trafficking) refers to the chattel slavery of Europeans, whether by non-Europeans (such as North Africans and the Muslim world), or by other Europeans (for example naval galley slaves or the Vikings' thralls). Slaves of European origin were present in ancient Rome in Greek history and the Ottoman Empire. Under Muslim rule, the Arab slave trades which had included Caucasian captives were often fuelled by raids into European territories or were taken as children in the form of a blood tax from the families of citizens of conquered territories to serve the empire for a variety of functions. It is believed that many Gypsies were first brought to Europe by the Muslims as their slaves. Gypsies were recorded as slaves as early as 430 when 12000 Gypsy dancers and musicians from a tribe of India were given as a gift to the court of the Sha of Persia king Bahran V. Ottoman advances resulted in many captive Christians as slaves being carried deep into Muslim territory. The Byzamtines from Afghanistan were said to have taken up to 27,000 prisoners as slaves when they conquered Anzarba from the valley of the lower Tigris and moved to lower Syria. These were said to be skilled workers in all types of craft with wood and engineering, performers and fortune tellers. They used these Gypsies as slaves to carry stolen treasures along with all their victorious spoils of war.These Gypsies were described as baptised heathens. They were of dark skin and wore Saracen style clothing and carried weapons. These captured Gypsies were believed to be workers with animals, silversmiths and entertainers. They included amongst them also broom makers, chimney sweeps, brick makers, musicians, dancers and bear leaders.

At the start of the 11th century King Muhmud of Ghazni used Roma slave warriors in his efforts to destroy all the Sindh and Punjab peoples in India. Gypsies who arrived in Romania were divided into groups such as those who were State owned, those owned by land owners or monasteries for work in the monasteries, the mines and the rivers. Whilst others were given as gifts to the aristocracy or else auctioned off on the many slave auctions blocks of that time. The state leaders were grateful for these slaves whilst so many of their countries men were away at war. They were used

3

as fresh labour to work the fields, along sides the prisoners of war, criminals and the peasants. Then following a great battle in 1192 AD it is believed that all these slaves were freed. With many of them beginning their long journeys of migration travelling towards Asia then into North Africa, then into Spain and eventually into the European continent. Throughout the next three centuries they were invaded by many armies such as those of Genghis Khan who had driven the Sinti Gypsy metal workers from their homeland in the Sind. The Mongol invasions and conquests in the 13th century took very many of their captives into slavery. The Mongols enslaved skilled individuals, as well as women and children and marched them to Karakonu whence they were sold throughout Eurasia. Many of them were also shipped to the slave market.The first evidence of the Roma Gypsies presence in contemporary Romania is mentioned in a document in 1385. Miria 1. (1382-1418) of Wallachia. When there was a transfer of forty tents sales of Gypsies by gift, not sale-made by his uncle Viad 1 to a monastery. This appears to support his belief that Gypsies were already slaves in the middle of the 1300s when thousands of these Gypsies families had been donated as gifts by the noblemen to the many Catholic monasteries in Serbia. They were referred to as being aţhiganoi or"heretics, profoundly derogatory terms which had its roots in the old Greek term Athiganoi -which translated means as 'untouchable, pagan, impure'. Thus giving them the status of a heretical sect. Upon arrival in the Byzantine Empire, Roma were considered members of this sect, and the term turned into a general one for any type of conduct or belief that deviated from institutionalized Christian norms. There are a great many documents that testify to all these many slave transactions. The Ottomans penetrated into Europe earlier in the 1350s and in 1382 the Golden Horde under Khan Tokhtamysh had ransacked Moscow, burning the city and carrying off thousands of inhabitants as slaves. Then later their capture of Constantinople (now Istanbul) in 1453 opened new floodgates for the slave-trade from the European front.

Contemporary chronicles note that the Ottomans reduced masses of the inhabitants of Greece, Romania, and the Balkans to slavery. Though when the Western Roman Empire fell in the 15th century, enslavement, which had been such an integral part of the empire's economy, began to be replaced by serfdom (an integral part of a feudal economy). Much attention is focused on the serf. His plight was not much better than the enslaved person's had been, as he was bound to the land instead of to an individual enslaver, and could not be sold to another estate. However, Gypsy enslavement didn't just disappear for as a Moldavian chronicle in 1471 stated that when Stephen defeated Prince Radu cel Frumos at Soci, "he took with him into slavery 17,000 Gypsies."

Roma slaves worked in the monasteries and mines alongside the Tatar and Ottoman prisoners of war, Romanian criminals and peasants. Others worked the rivers and out in the countryside. With so many of the male population away fighting in war the state was thankful for this new influx of Gypsy slave labour, which they used for harvesting or the collection of minerals for their wars. Roma made it much more of a widespread practice.For almost five centuries, the Romas slave labour resulted in huge earnings for their masters: landowners, the feudal aristocracy and the Orthodox Church. Romani people's status was that of subjugated people. They were the absolute property of their masters: their masters' personality, faith and habits dictated their whole existence. Between 1414 and 1423, some 10,000 eastern European slaves were sold in Venice. During these times Prince Vlad of Wallace transported 12000 persons who were deemed or looked like Egyptians Gypsies from Bulgaria for slave labour. Conservative tabulation of the slave raids against the Eastern European population indicate that at least 7 Million White European people, men, women and children were enslaved by Muslims and that between 1436-1442, some 500,000 people were seized in the Balkans. Many of the captives died in forced marches towards Anatolia (Turkey).In 1452 Pope Nicholas V issued the papal ull Dum Divers as, granting Afonso V of Portugal the right to reduce any "Saracens, pagans and any other unbelievers" to hereditary slavery which legitimized slave trade under Catholic beliefs of that time. These papal bulls came to serve as a justification for the subsequent era of the slave trade and European colonialism. The European slave-trade continued at a pace, from then and well into the 1700s, Europeans from Italy, Spain, Portugal, France, and England were sold into slavery by North Africans.

Gypsy slaves were sold at auction blocks. With slave traders selling slaves in lots of up to 500 slaves. Once they were bought they became the personal property of their owners whose only obligation was to clothe and feed them. The slaves were put to work or else exchanged for other goods or commodities. Roma slaves were divided into three categories: 1) Those owned or belonging to the lord: 2) Those belonging to the monasteries and: 3) Those belonging to the boyars. Slaves were often status symbols with the slave-master's social standing often being rated by the number and kinds of skilled slaves he owned. A visitor to one of the slave estates wrote- "The landowner had all that he needed on his estate: cooks, bakers, gardeners, masons, shoemakers, blacksmiths, musicians, labourers, all of them Tziganes (Gypsies)". Thousands of these Gypsies had been cruelly treated by their boyar masters with a wide range of horrific punishments were carried out against them for no more than some mere minor petty crime. The range of horrific punishments which were inflicted on them were great and included being shackled, branded, flaying the soles of feet with whips, cutting off of lips, noses and ears, and forced to wear spiked collars or raped, tortured or flogged to death. A reformer of that period commented on the slavery which he had witnessed in Iasi stated: "Human being's wearing chains on their arms and legs, others with iron clamp's round their foreheads".The Bukovina Austrian authorities were initially horrified by the way that slaves were treated by the newly settled refugee slave-masters. But these slave-masters were allowed by the authorities to continue this practice, provided such activities took place privately and not in the public domain. Male house slaves were castrated so as not to present a threat to noblewoman of the house.The diary of Felix Colson, a French journalist, recounts his travels to the Balkans and states: "Although it frequently happens, not one boyar was on trial for murdering a Gypsy in his possession." Djuvara notes that the usual treatment of Gypsy slaves was demeaning whilst local people all believed the masters words. That one could not get anything out of the Gypsies without using a whip. Gypsy slaves could be exchanged for animals such as pigs. They were made into clowns but were also social status symbols.

A defective Gypsy slave could even be exchanged for a jar of honey. Romanian noblemen felt entitled to buy and sell bondsmen, as any other commodity, and so the Roma had become comparable with any valuable object. They were given as dowry at weddings or offered to monasteries in exchange for the mentioning of their former masters' name during mass. They were passed on from father to son whilst some traders could even sale up to 500 slaves at a time. A female slave's value was often dependent on her class. Many young slave girls were used as property whilst extra-marital relationships between male slave owners and female slaves were common practice with many illegitimate children from these being also kept as slaves. Young Gypsy attractive girls being used as property and often these were treated worse than animals.These Slaves could marry only with the consent of their owners, usually through a financial agreement which resulted in the selling of one slave to the other owner or through an exchange. With no agreement the couple were split and their children were divided between the two slaveholders. Marriage between a free person and a slave was initially possible but only by the free person becoming a slave. Although later it was possible for a free person to keep one's social status with children resulting from the marriage also being free. During his lifetime or in his will a slave owner had the power to free his slaves. But such instances were rather rare and those that were freed often selling themselves to monasteries or boyars in order to survive.

The Muslim Ottoman Empire enslaved up to 1,250,000bo white slaves in the North African Barbary States. These slaves were Ukrainians, Georgians, Circassians, Greeks, Armenians, Bulgarians, Romanians, British and Slavs, etc. As an example, Ottoman forces retreated from Vienna with 80,000 slaves in 1683. Their Ottoman rulers preferred white female sex slaves for their Harems in Constantinople (Istanbul) and elsewhere. Britain's Lundy Island was a Muslim Slave Trade colony to capture English people for enslavement during the 1600s.

For years, there had been frequent raids on the Russian principalities for slaves and to plunder towns. Russian chronicles record about 40 raids by Kazan Khans on the Russian territories in the first half of the 16th century alone. In 1621 several Englishmen, being captured and carried into Algiers, were sold as slaves. These are the words of one put on board of their number.

"We were hurried like dogs into the market, where men sell hackneys in England. we were tossed up and down to see who would give most for us and although we had heavy hearts but looked sad continences, yet many came to behold us, us by the hand, sometimes turning us round about, sometimes feeling our brawny and naked arms, and so so beholding our prices written in our breasts. they bargained for us accordingly and at last we were all sold". Shortly afterwards several were put onboard an Algerine corsair to serve as slaves. In their last attempt to overrun Europe in 1683, the Ottoman army, although defeated, returned from the Gates of Vienna with 80,000 captives. As a result a great number of slaves flowed into the Islamic slave markets.

The commerce in white Christian slaves flourished all over Europe in the early 17th century as William Atkins in 1622 described how he and some other English Catholic school boys bound for Seville were despite being encouraged to fight by a drought of aquivit mixed with gunpowder, captured by a Morisco captain in the service of the king of Morocco. He was imprisoned with 800 Spanish, French, Portugese, Italian, Irish and Flemish slaves in Sale, on the Atlantic coast, near what is now Rabat, where slaves were sold in the streets with sellers calling out," Who will buy a slave"? and the captives being beaten to walk faster by a peevil, which was a bulls penis. These slaves were treated with as least as much brutality as the African slaves were by the Europeans. 800 English men were held captive as slaves at Sale in 1625,over 1,500 in 1626.

CHAPTER TWO

GYPSY AND WHITE SLAVES

Romani People

Exodus freedoms from invading lands
conscripting soldiers with weapons in hands
fleeing the countries fleeing the lands
Romani peoples of pure Gypsy bands

Ray Wills

They hung the man and flog the woman
who steal the goose from off the common
but leave the greater villain loose
who steal the common from the goose

Poem of Protest 1764

INTUITIVE GYPSY ROMA

The third eye intuition dictates
the fortune tellers contemplates
insightful, precise and origins of the east
the cards of wisdoms reading
with bells on their feet

Tents and drapes and occult themes
wisdoms stories myths and man-kinds dreams
the oracle and the eyes and themes
that gaze that look into the stars
the dark mysterious worlds of wonder faith and space

Tattoos and song all rich in tone
nomadic life of Indian home
past and future in one look
wise and rich in histories traditional past
insightful wisdoms in love of their craft

Ray Wills

WHITE SLAVERY IN THE EAST—GOING TO THE SLAVE-MARKET.

Maanier Hoe de Gevange Kristen Slaven uit Algiers verkoft werden.

11

The vast majority of historical books covering accounts of slavery will avoid the term "White slaves" when referring to none blacks. Such historians will go around the subject as if it white slavery itself did not exist. Instead they choose to or prefer to use terms such as European slaves, Christian slaves and the phrase blacks slaves and the others.

Most governments today do not teach White Slavery in their World History classes. Children of modern times are only taught about the Black African slave trade. There is also no mention of British Gypsies in the official history books on the slave trade. No mention of those hordes of white slaves which were taken from Britain to America. Huge numbers of Gypsies were also taken as slaves from Portugal and Spain in irons and chains to American colonies and Africa.

In the earliest part of the Middle Ages, enslaved people could be found in many societies, among them the Cymry in Wales and the Anglo-Saxons in England. The Slavs of central Europe were often captured and sold into enslavement, usually by rival Slavonic tribes. Moors were known to enslave people and believed that setting an enslaved person free was an act of great piety. Christians also enslaved, bought, and sold enslaved people, as evidenced by the following:

When the Bishop of Le Mans transferred a large estate to the Abbey of St. Vincent in 572, 10 enslaved people went with it.

Pope Gregory in the sixth century first witnessed blonde hair, blue eyed boys awaiting sale in a Roman slave market. The Romans enslaved thousands of white inhabitants of Great Britain, who were also known as Angles. Pope Gregory was very interested in the looks of these boys therefore asking their origin. He was told they were Angles from Briton. Gregory stated, "Non Angli, sed Angeli." (Not Angles but Angels.

In the seventh century, the wealthy Saint Eloi bought British and Saxon enslaved people in batches of 50 and 100 so that he could set them free. A transaction between Ermedruda of Milan, and a gentleman by the name of Totone, recorded the price of 12 new gold solidi for an enslaved boy (referred to as "it" in the record). Twelve solidi were much less than the cost of a horse. The between the eighth to the eleventh centuries proved to be very profitable for Rouen France. Rouen was the transfer point of Irish and Flemish slaves to the Arabian nations. The major component of slave trade in the eleventh century were the Vikings. They spirited many 'Irish' to Spain, Scandinavia and Russia. Legends have it; some 'Irish' may have been taken as far as Constantinople.

The French were involved in the early 9th century, the Abbey of St. Germain des Prés listed 25 of their 278 householders as enslaved people. The Italian ambassador Liutprand of Cremona, as one example in the 10th century, presented a gift of four eunuchs to EmperorConstantineV11.Pope Gregory reputedly made the pun, Non Angli, sed Angeli("Not Angles, but Angels"), following a response to his query regarding the identity of a group of fair-haired slaves.In the turmoil at the end of the Avignon Papacy, the Florentines engaged in insurrection against the pope. Gregory XI excommunicated the Florentines and ordered them to be enslaved wherever taken. The city of Verdun had become the centre of the thriving European slave trade of young boys. These youngsters were sold to the Islamic emirates of Ibenia where they were enslaved as eunuchs. Ireland and Denmark provided markets for captured Anglo-Saxon and Celtic slaves. Slavery during these years was mainly in the hands of Venetian and Genoa merchants and cartels, who were involved in the slave trade. In the 12th Century thousands of Gypsy families were donated as gifts by the noblemen to the many Catholic monasteries in Serbia, or auctioned at slave auction blocks.

Ruth Mazo Karras Norwegian Vikings made slave raids not only against the Irish and Scots (who were often called Irish in Norse sources) but also against Norse settlers in Ireland or Scottish Isles or even in Norway itself slave trading was a major commercial activity of the Viking Age. The children of the White slaves in Iceland were routinely murdered en masse".

Gypsy history is a series of expulsions, beginning with their exodus out of India, across Persia, into the Balkans 'till they were swept to the edge of the European continent, over gangplanks, onto ships sending them to the Americas. Their banishment and transportation was prominent throughout Europe during the 15th century and throughout the 16th century. As more and more Gypsies poured into Europe brutal laws were passed as a means to repress and control them. Enslaved women taken after the fall of Capua in 1501 were put up for sale in Rome.. In Spain, the Gitanos were whipped, burnt or branded during a period of over 100 years. These included 200,000 from South Russia (1555), 100,000 from Moscow. Spain shipped Gypsies to the Americas in the 1400s; three were transported by Columbus to the Caribbean on his third voyage in 1498. In 1488, King Ferdinand sent 100 Moorish enslaved people to Pope Innocent VIII, who presented them as gifts to his cardinals and other court notables. In 1499 King Charles expelled all Gypsies from Spain, under penalty of enslavement. During the same period in Spain, according to a decree issued in 1538, Gypsies were enslaved for perpetuity to individuals as a punishment for escaping. King Philip III of Spain ordered all Gypsies (who were called Gitanos) out of Spain in 1619, this time under penalty of death. An exception was granted for those who would settle down in one place, dress as Spaniards, and stop speaking their ancient language.Other Europeans countries followed suit by continuing the banishment of Gypsies including Portugal who banned Gypsies in 1526, and any of them born there were deported to the Portuguese African colonies Denmark in 1536, Moraia 1538.Scotland 1541.In Norway in 1544 when some Gypsies appeared, they were said to be those prisoners whom the English had got rid of by forcibly embarking them throwing them overboard from ships. Poland 1557, Venitia 1549,1558 and 1588.

The King of France, Charles IX, banned Gypsies in 1561, and ordered that any Gypsy man caught in France be sentenced to three years on the galleys, in spite of the fact that they were pronounced a non-violent people.

In 1633 King Philip Iv of France lowered the penalties. In 1657 some Gypsies ended up in being sold as slaves to Constantinople sold by Venetians.

King Phillip V in 1665 issued a decree that demanded that all unemployed Gypsies men between the ages of 20 and 50 years be sent as galley slaves. He later changed this decree to that all Gypsy men had to row in the galleys saying that.. "There is a great need for galley men and rowers and everywhere there is an excess of this odious race, who are all spies, thieves and liars."By 1666, Gypsy men were condemned to the galleys—this time for life—and Gypsy women caught in France had their heads shaved. The officer in charge of the galley slaves in Marseilles wrote: "I would like a decision to be made to take the lazy, the pilgrims, the Gypsies, and other wanderers and fill up whole galleys with them. That would clean the world of its burdensome filth." Thus, under the pretext of maintaining public order, Gypsies and paupers were recruited... King Edward VI passed a law stating that Gypsies be "branded with a V on their breast, and then enslaved for two years," and if they escaped and were recapture.All Gypsies were expelled by the Holy Roman Empire and the Holy Catholic church. In 1564 Pope Pius V expelled all those known as Gypsies from the Roman Catholic church. This was a truly important event in their history as it was to brand them as being non Christian and as a wicked peoples. They were expelled from Germany by the holy Roman for espenage. Elector Achilles of Brandenburgh had banned the Sinti from his land.

Any non Sinti had the right to hunt Gypsies, flog them, incarcerate or kill them, many other countries soon followed suit with similar actions. With Switzerland bringing in the death penalty. The Spanish nobility until then had protected the Gypsies at first. It was there that Gypsy women were adored for their beauty and seductive charms; Gypsy men were admired as excellent judges of the quality of horses, and hired by nobles to procure them for their stables. d, they were then branded with an S and made slaves for life.

In 1571, the Crimean Tatars attacked and sacked Moscow, burning everything but the Kremlin and taking thousands of captives as slaves. In Crimea, about 75% of the population consisted of slaves. With a minimum of 25,000 white slaves at any time in Sultan Moulay Ismail's palace, records Ahmed ez-Zayyani; Algiers maintained a population of 25,000 white slaves between 1550 and 1730. From 1575 to 1676, the Tatars captured over 130000 Ukrainians; in numerous raids. Some were ransomed, but most were sold into slavery. The Tartars and other Black Sea peoples had sold millions of Ukrainians, Georgians, Circassians, Greeks, Armenians, Bulgarians, Slavs and Turks," which received little notice. The Tatar slave-raiding Khans returned with 18,000 slaves from Poland (1463), 100,000 from Lvov (1498), 60,000 from South Russia (1515), 50,000–100,000 from Galicia (1516), during the 'harvesting of the steppe.' Numbers from Moscow (1521) 400,000 were taken. 800,000 from Moscow (1521).

- B. D Davis

According to the Egerton manuscript, British Museum, the enactment of 1652: it may be lawful for two or more justices of peace within any county, city or town, corporate belonging to the commonwealth to from time to time by warrant cause to be apprehended, seized on and detained all and every person or persons that shall be found begging and vagrant in any town, parish or place to be conveyed into the Port of London, or unto any other port from where such person or persons may be shipped into a foreign colony or plantation. Gypsy women were more likely to be sold as slaves then gypsy men.

In 1674 Master Drew wrote of gypsies. That" they were a lazy and idle sort of people which cannot endure to take pains for an honest livelihood but rather than labour up and down all the summer time in droves or companies". Russian agricultural slaves were formally converted into serfdom in 1679 and whole groups of Gypsies were sent to Brazil in 1686. In 1699 B.E. Gent classed Gypsies with beggars thieves and cheats.

The 'official' persecution of gypsies began in France in the early sixteenth century and reached a peak with Louis XIV decree of 1682 which ordered gypsy men to serve in the galleys in perpetuity, women to have their heads shaved, or, if persistent, gypsies to be flogged and banished, and children to be ensconced in poor houses.

Jean Louis Parrant, who was in Moldavia during the French revolution, when referring to Gypsies asks himself: 'What can be said about this numerous miserable flock of beings (because they can't be otherwise described) that are called Gypsies and are lost for the humanity, placed on the same level with the cattle of burden and often treated even worse by the their barbaric master whose revolting (so-called) property they are?'. They were born slaves; that every child born from a slave mother was a slave; that their masters had power of life and death over them; that each owner had the right to sell or offer his slaves; In Spain more than ten thousand Roma were rounded up in a well planned military-police action one day in 1749. The purpose according to a leading clergyman who advised the government was to 'root out this bad race, which is hateful to God and pernicious to man'. The result was devastating to the Roma community – the deportations, detentions, forced labour and killings destroyed much of the original Roma culture.

In the Austro-Hungarian Empire the rulers applied a policy of enforced assimilation. Roma children were taken from their parents and no Roma was allowed to marry another Roma and Romani language was banned. This policy was brutally enforced. For instance, the use of the 'Gypsy' language was to be punishable by flogging. In the East European country of Romania, land of iron-fisted ruler Prince Vlad Tepes, Gypsies were being systematically rounded up and enslaved. He brought back nearly 12,000 Gypsy slaves from campaigns in Bulgaria during his reign. Gypsy slaves just like the African slaves a few years later were sold on the block to the highest bidder. There were cases when Gypsies were sold according to their weight, exchanged for honey barrels, pawned off, or offered as presents. Milhail Kogalnicearnu, a former Romanian politician remembers seeing people "being with hands and feet enchained, with iron circles around their forehead or metal collar around their neck. Bloody whips and other punishments such as starvation, hanging over a burning fire, the detention barrack and the forcing to stay naked in snow or in the frozen water of a river-this is the treatment applied to the miserable Gypsies." Legislative texts, referring to Gypsies under a double denomination-Gypsies or bondsmen-stated that they were born slaves; that every child born from a slave mother was a slave; that their masters had power of life and death over them; that owners had the right to sell or offer his slaves; and that every masterless Gypsy is propriety of the state. Romany people were flogged, burned with lye and made to wear a three cornered spiked iron collar. Many Gypsies were marked with a letter G on their forehead others had a letter V on their chests. These Gypsy slaves were considered to be the personal property of their masters and owners. They would be put to work, sold them or even exchanged them for goods and commodities. The masters could punish their slaves physically via beatings, whippings or imprisonment. But he or she did not hold the power of the death sentence over them. Their only obligation however was to feed and clothe them whilst they worked for them at their manor or place of residence.

Comte d'Antraigues observed that for almost five centuries, the Gypsies slave labour resulted in huge earnings for their masters: landowners, who were the feudal aristocracy and the Orthodox Church. Romani people were the absolute property of their masters. Roma bondsmen were subjected to atrocious treatment. Gypsy slaves as punishments wore a collar fitted with iron spikes on the inside that prevented the wearer from lying down to rest. The squires are their absolute masters. They sell or kill them like cattle, at their sole discretion. Their children are born slaves with no distinction on sex- Comte d' Antraigues.

The abolishment of Roma slavery began with young aristocrat Romanians leaving to study in Western Europe. Upon returning home, they gave voice to progressive ideas denouncing slavery. At the same time, Western Europe, and France especially, exerted considerable pressure on the newly formed Romanian state regarding the abolition of slavery and that every masterless Gypsy is propriety of the state. Romanian noblemen felt entitled to buy and sell bondsmen, as any other commodity, and so the Roma became comparable with any valuable object. They were given as dowry at weddings or offered to monasteries in exchange for the mentioning of their former masters' name during mass. Bondsmen

18

auctions, similar to public markets, were kept track of in court records and announced in newspapers.

The boyars pleaded their case to the Bukovina and Galicia authorities, claiming that the banning of slavery was a transgression against the autonomy and traditions of the province and that such bondage was the appropriate state for the Roma and was for their own good. The Romanian Orthodox monasteries were opposed to any order to abolish slavery by Joseph II, Holy Roman Emperor, on June 19th, 1783 in Czernowitz.

In Hungary in 1782 forty-one gypsies in one area were barbarically executed, on charges of cannibalism and the remainder were driven into marshes where they perished. Soldiers captured gypsy children and young couples and dragged them off, oblivious to the pleas of distraught parents, many of whom committed suicide in their despair.

In Romania 1839 there were up to a quarter of a million Tzigani Gypsy slaves. The Bucharest papers of 1845 announced the sale of 200 families of Gypsies, who had belonged to the late Serdar Nika, they added that they would be sold at a ducat less than usual, as not less than five families must be taken at a time. Though six years later it was made illegal in Wallachia to dispose of more than three families at once or to separate families when sold. These sales must have existed for centuries. Many of these Gypsies then were travellers in tents in the summer and settled in caves during winter months.

A prime lot of Gypsy slaves, to be sold by auction at the Monastery of St. Elias, 8 May 1852, consisting of 18 men, 10 boys, 7 women and 3 girls: in fine condition."Wallachia.

In 1852, a Bill of Sale was placed in the Bucharest newspaper *Luna* by St. Elias Monastery and advertised the auction of thirty eight men, women and children as items of property. Whilst the abolitionist movement in Britain had finally concluded the Transatlantic Slave Trade in 1807, slavery of the Roma in Wallachia, Transylvania and Moldavia, which later became

Romania, continued until 1856 and continued in practice for decades after. Similar to the British government slave reparations, compensation was paid to the slave owners for loss of property rather than the slaves themselves. Furthermore, the slaves had to settle in the same village or estate where they had been enslaved for a further two censuses and pay their taxes to the compensation fund for their ex-owners. Complete legal freedom was not realised until 1864. Most slaves found themselves with nowhere to go but back to working for their masters in return for room and board, essentially reinstating their serfdom in practice if not in law. Those who turned to nomadism escaped the social engineering policies implemented after the abolition which scattered some of the 250,000 freed Roma across villages in Romania, banned Romany language, enforced compulsory re-education for children and insisted on the label *emancipat* to refer to freed gypsies.

Then in 1855 /1856 the Moldavian and Wallachian Assemblies voted unanimously to abolish slavery and serfdom within their principalities with complete legal freedom following in 1864.

Many Roma returned to work on their former masters estates now as free persons. Others settled in villages under the supervision of the local police or joined the nomadic Roma craftsmen and musicians in some areas of the country.The Romnichels or English Gypsies, had began to come to the United States from England in 1850. Their arrival coincided with an increase in the demand for draft horses in agriculture and then in urbanization, and many Romnichels worked as horse-traders. After the rapid decline in the horse trade following the First World War, most Romnichels relied on previously secondary enterprises, "basket-making," including the manufacture and sale of rustic furniture, and fortune-telling. Horse and mule trading continued to some extent in southern states where poverty and terrain slowed the adoption of tractor power (Salo and Salo 1982).The Rom also arrived in the United States from Serbia, Russia and Austria-Hungary beginning in the 1880's, part of the larger wave of immigration from southern and eastern Europe in the late 19th and early 20th centuries.

Primary immigration ended, for the most part, in 1914, with the beginning of the First World War and subsequent tightening of immigration restrictions (Salo and Salo 1986).

Many people in this group specialized in coppersmith work mainly the repair and re-tinning of industrial equipment used in bakeries, laundries, confectioneries, and other businesses. The Rom, too, developed the fortune-telling business in urban areas.

The Ludar or "Romanian Gypsies," also came to the United States during the great immigration from southern and eastern Europe between 1880 and 1914. They also came to America during World War I 1914-1918 and World War II 199-1945. Most of them settled in the metropolitan area of Barranquilla. Several groups, all known to outsiders as "Gypsies," live today in the United States. In their native languages, each of the groups refers to itself by a specific name, but all translate their self-designations as "Gypsy" when speaking English. Each had its own cultural, linguistic, and historical tradition before coming to this country, and each maintains social distance from the others. In the United States they continued as musicians to the Hungarian and Slovak immigrant settlements, and count the musical tradition as a basic cultural element. The sparse literature on this group begins in 1921. Curiously the proportion of scholarly efforts is higher than for the literature on other groups: three sociological studies (although two are unpublished master's theses), and one survey focused on music. In Romania a campaign began to convince the wealthy slaveholders to also free their slaves. It was influenced by the anti-slavery movement in the United States and was also given strength by newspaper anti-slavery campaigns and Harriet Beecher Stowe's book famous 'Uncle Tom's Cabin'.An Afro-Gypsy community today lives in St. Martin's Parish, and reportedly there is another one in central Cuba, both descended from intermarriage between the two enslaved peoples.Australia was the preferred destination for Romanichal transportation, as it's use as a penal colon. Its believed that three Romanichal were present on the first Australian fleet, one of it was thought to be one James Squire who went on to successfully found Australia's first commercial brewery in 1798. His grandson James Farnell was to become the first native-born

Premier of New South Wales in 1877. The Irish Travellers immigrated, like the Romnichels, from the mid to late nineteenth century. They specialized in the horse and mule trade, as well as in itinerant sales of goods and services; the latter gained in importance after the demise of the horse and mule trade. The literature also refers to this group as Irish Traders or, sometimes, Tinkers. Their ethnic language is referred to in the literature as Irish Traveller Cant. The popular literature on Irish Travellers includes articles in Catholic periodicals. The present population of Scottish Travellers in North America also dates from about 1850, although the 18th-century transportation records appear to refer to this group. Unlike that of the other groups, Scottish Traveller immigration has been continuous. Also unlike the other groups, Scottish Travellers have continued to travel between Scotland and North America, as well as between Canada and the United States, after immigration. Scottish Travellers also engaged in horse trading, but since the first quarter of the 20th century have specialized in itinerants.

CHAPTER THREE

THE BRITISH GYPSIES IN SLAVERY

They hung the poor Gypsies or sold them as slaves
they tortured them daily from birth to their graves
they sent them to prison or the US of A
where they gave them some land
then made them work all the day

They marked them with signs
on their heads and their breasts
just because they were different and not like the rest
with the rings on their fingers and their dark shiny hair
though their music was rich and they worked at the fairs

They gave them sites in the war years
when they fought for this land
then they moved them on later with their ponies and bands
they made them take houses and to give up their ways
and to live in this country for the rest of their days

Ray Wills

The Gypsy travelling community has been in Britain for at least 500 years or more, but their origins and history is often difficult to trace. Misunderstandings of Roma culture created suspicions and fears, which in turn led to rampant speculation, stereotypes, and biased stories. Many of these stereotypes and stories are still rampant in our society today.Attempts to assimilate Roma into society involved stealing their children and placing them with other families; giving them cattle and feed, expecting them to become farmers; outlawing their customs, language, and clothing; and forcing them to attend school and church. A huge range of Decrees, Acts, laws, and mandates often allowed the killing of Roma people who for generations were seen as no more than vagrants. They were seen as wicked, unlawful, thieves and tyrants. For many this meant that just to be a Gypsy was punishable with hangings, imprisonment, transportation and slavery Slavery had existed in 9th and 10th Century in the west of Britain with many Cornish slave owners not setting their slaves free and they were routinely bought and sold. Though slavery was never a major economic factor in the British Isles during the Middle Ages.After the Norman Conquest of 1066, the law no longer supported chattel slavery and slaves became part of the larger body of serfs. Though all of this was common practice most crimes committed were due to poverty for to survive.

Gypsies, have lived in the Americas since 1498, when Columbus brought some on his third voyage to the West Indies. Their subsequent forced transportation brought most Gypsies across the Atlantic.According to Ian Hancock- Oliver Cromwell shipped Romanichal Gypsies (i.e.,Gypsies from Britain) as slaves to the southern plantations). There is documentation of Gypsies being owned by freed black slaves in Jamaica, and in both Cuba and Louisiana today there are Afro -Romani populations resulting from intermarriage between freed African and Gypsy slaves.It still remains an untold fact that, the majority of the early slaves to the New World were actually white. The Church of England owned many slaves via the Anglican Church's Society for the Propagation of the Gospel in Foreign Parts. These slaves worked on their many sugar plantations in the West Indies. The established Church was

24

very much involved in the slave trade throughout history. With the Catholic Orthodox Church and Church of England Anglican Church being major slaveholders and as a result they were not opposed to the institution of slavery.Throughout the centuries numerous Acts were enacted by the Monarchy and Church establishments to deal with the problem of the Gypsies. Many cruel and barbaric measures were taken including their banishment, imprisonment, transportation, enslavement and executions. Many Gypsies from England, Scotland and Ireland were deported to America and the West Indies as slaves. The slaves master had the right to force a slave to do any work, no matter how vile, with whip and chains. If the slave is absent for a fortnight, he is condemned to slavery for life and is to be branded on forehead or back with the letter S; if he runs away three times, he is to be executed as a felon. If it happens that a vagabond has been idling about for three days, he is to be taken to his birthplace, branded with a red hot iron with the letter V on his breast, and set to work, in chains, on the roads or at some other labour. Every master may put an iron ring round the neck, arms or legs of his slave, by which to know him more easily. At the beginning of the 1500s, monasteries were opening in European cities, the monks brought with them their Roma slaves. Gypsies were now well established in Europe during this period. With very many of them slaves throughout countries such as Rumania, Spain, Portugal, Russia and Hungary as well to a lesser extent in other European countries. Many Gypsies were victimised by the state in England and punitive and restrictive laws continued. Gypsies were also frowned upon and condemned by practically all of the countries and states of Europe. Plus new laws across Europe were to be introduced later by kings and principalities which made the Gypsy Travellers life perilous. As a result many Gypsies had been executed, tortured or transported as slaves from England to the new worlds of Northern America, Australia and the West Indies Barbados and Jamaica etc.In England Henry VIII Egyptian Act of 1530 was passed as a means to expel Gypsies from the realm within 16 days on pin of imprisonment and seizure of goods for being lewd vagabonds, conning the good citizens out of their money, and committing a rash of felony robberies. Henry decreed that "there should be] whipping and imprisonment for sturdy vagabonds. They are to be tied to the cart-tail and whipped until the blood streams from their bodies, then they are to swear on oath to go back to their birthplace or to serve where they have lived the last three years and to 'put themselves to labour'. For the second arrest for vagabondage the whipping is to be repeated and half the ear sliced off; but for the third relapse the offender is to be executed as a hardened criminal and enemy of the common weal." Many Gypsies were hung or imprisoned. The Egyptians Act was aimed at ridding the country of all those known as Egyptians or Gypsies, by banning immigration and 'voluntarily' requiring Gypsies to leave the country within sixteen days. The punishment for those who did not conform was the confiscation of goods and property, imprisonment and deportation (Mayall 1995). England began to deport Romanichal Gypsies to Norway, a process that was continued and encouraged by both Queen Elizabeth I and King James I. The Vagrancy Act of 1547 stated that any able-bodied person who was out of work for more than three days should be branded with a V and sold into slavery for two years. Other offences by the same individual would lead to a life of slavery. Though many local authorities refused to enact this harsh legislation. Under the Act vagabonds could face enslavement as bonded slaves for two years. The Act still continued containing the earlier 1536 provision that Gypsy children should be put to service. Work to be provided for the aged poor. The later Egyptian Act of 1554 directed that Gypsies must abandon their naughty vile and idle and ungodly life and company and adopt a settled lifestyle. They would then not be punished, however the punishment was extended to include execution for those not complying. Queen Mary I made it a crime to be an immigrant Romanichal Gypsy, laws were passed to condemning all Gypsies to death. The Marian Act accused Gypsies of 'such abominable living as is not in any Christian realm to be permitted'. Gypsies, however, remained exposed to the vagrancy laws and were frequently arrested for 'not giving a good account of themselves'. This law was aimed at ridding the country of all Egyptians or Gypsies, by banning immigration and 'voluntarily' requiring Gypsies to leave the country within sixteen days. The punishment for those who did not conform or comply was the confiscation of goods and property, imprisonment and deportation

(Mayall 1995).In August of 1559 during the reign of Queen Elizabeth 1st a very large number of Gypsies were stopped and detained in Dorchester Dorset. They were sent to trial before the Lord Liutenant of Dorset. He having heeded an order by the Queen instructing him that they the Gypsies should be made an example with some of them to be executed, In September they went to trial but were however released, due to the fact that they had journeyed from Scotland and not as originally thought from overseas. Another law passed in England by Queen Elizabeth 1 in 1562 forced Gypsies to settle into permanent dwellings, or face death. It made it illegal even to be a Gypsy ('those calling themselves Egyptians') and throughout history the poor with no fixed abode or occupation had been, at best, viewed with deep suspicion.The Elizabethan 1 statute of 1563 States 'for the punishment of vagabonds calling themselves Egyptians', it recognised Gypsies as native subjects, but criminalised anyone 'seen or found' in their company, 'or counterfeiting, transforming or disguising themselves by their apparel, speech or other behaviour like unto such vagabonds'. Queen Elizabeth 1 expelled Gypsies along with all freed black slaves. Laws were passed condemning all Gypsies to death. Queen Elizabeth 1 later introduced the Vagrancy Act 1572. which defined a rogue as a person who had no land, no master, and no legitimate trade or source of income; it included rogues in the class of vagrants or vagabonds. If a person were apprehended as a rogue, he would be stripped to the waist, whipped until bleeding, and a hole, about the compass of an inch about, would be burned through the cartilage of his right ear with a hot iron. A rogue who was charged with a second offence, unless taken in by someone who would give him work for one year, could face execution. A rogue charged with a third offence would only escape death if someone hired him for two years.

The Vagrancy Act had decreed that "unlicensed beggars above fourteen years of age are to be severely flogged and branded on the left ear unless someone will take them into service for two years; in case of a repetition of the offence, if they are over eighteen, they are to be executed, unless someone will take them into service for two years; but for the third offence they are to be executed without

27

mercy as felons." The same act laid the legal groundwork for the enforced exile penal transportation of "obdurate idlers" to "such parts beyond the seas as shall be […] assigned by the Privy Council. At the time, this meant exile for a fixed term to the plantations in the Americas.

The King James 1st 1597 Vagrancy Act, banished and transplanted "incorrigible and dangerous rogues" overseas. This was known as "The Vagabonds Act", it provided penal transportation as a punishment for the very first time Under James I, England had began to deport Gypsy people to the American colonies, as well as Jamaica and Barbados. Dumping undesirables into the colonies became a widespread practice, not only Gypsies, but also "thieves, beggars, and whores. " European countries also forced the further transportation of the British Romani to the Americas. Anyone found to be wandering about and begging is declared a rogue and a vagabond. Justices of the peace in petty sessions were authorised to have them publicly whipped and for the first offence to imprison them for 6 months, for the second offence for 2 years. Whilst in prison they are to be whipped as much and as often as the justices of the peace think fit. Incorrigible and dangerous rogues are to be branded with an R on the left shoulder and set to hard labour, and if they are caught begging again, to be executed without mercy. Many Gipsies were banished to the America in colonial times, from England, Wales, Scotland and Ireland. Sometimes for merely being 'by habit and repute' Gipsies, is beyond dispute. The earliest actual document known dates from the time of the administration of Oliver Cromwell's successor, his son Richard, when the first trans-Atlantic expulsion of Gypsies was instituted: Large numbers of Gypsies were transported from Britain to the USA and Caribbean during these times. The most complete list of gypsies sentenced to transportation appears in "Directory of Scots Banished to the American Plantations, 1650-1775", by David Dobson,1984,Baltimore, MD Genealogical Publishing Co. includes 16 Scottish Travellers forming 3 groups sentenced in 1682, 1715 and 1739.

There were far more Gypsies in Barbados than at any other Caribbean island such as Jamaica which had its owns trade deal

28

with the Dutch traders and Levellers from England. However, while the designations Gypsy, Gyptian, Egyptian, &c, turn up in the records of transportation located in Britain, nothing similar appears anywhere in the documents examined in Barbados.

However an examination of the lists of those transported found in these works and in the Barbados Records indicated that a great number of individuals bearing Romanichal (British Gypsy) surnames did in fact arrive in Barbados: The names occurring include Boswell, Cook/Cooke, Hern/Herne/Heron, Lee/Leek, Locke, Palmer, Penfold/Pinfold, Price, Scot/Scott, Smith and Ward, ranging from one Pinfold to nine Boswells to over a hundred Smiths. Though all may not have been Gypsies Sometimes, a further clue was provided by the county of origin of the individual, where given (Cookes from Middlesex and Kent), or by occupation (Boswell, a blacksmith), but these must also be considered non-conclusive.Numerous commentators put the figure of those who were transported for numerous range of offences way above the official figure of 45,000. More than likely it exceeded 50,000.No doubt thousands of these, particularly in the case of Gypsies were transported for no more than being vagrants who did not normally appear in the official lists. Barbadian planters initially used white British labourers as indentured servants to work on their estates. Then from the middle of the 1600s onward, these planters began to purchase ever more enslaved workers to supplement and, eventually, to replace indentured labourers.The forcible removal of Gypsies from Britain to the West Indies or America is hardly mentioned in literature today. Yet is is true that they were. Those who returned unlawfully from their place of exile faced death by hanging. In 1603 an Order of Council was made for the transportation of Romancihal Gypsies from England to Newfoundland. Many went from the Dorset docks of Weymouth and Poole for these were great trading harbours to Newfoundland at the time. Such trade made many local traders very rich and throughout the Georgian age. Regular trips to Africa to purchase people to be sold into slavery were taking place by the 1620s. However, the trips were expensive, and the people had to be purchased.According to Robert Dawson a number of documents by

Macritchie and Chambers Scottish gypsies were taken to the plantations during these years, though not all the Gypsies completed their journeys there. It is estimated that during the 17th century of those several thousand Gypsies who were sent to the colonies most of these were sent to Barbados. Beir estimated that several thousands Gypsies were shipped there on slave ships in the 17th century alone. Most of them as punishment for just being Gypsies.

During those years most Gypsies were being expelled and cruel harsh laws continued to be enacted against them. Unemployment was rife and Gypsies were seen as scapegoats with high prices and peasants losing their jobs on the land. Gypsies stood out as being very different in appearance as well as in their ways and customs. Throughout the period from the 1600-1800s Gypsies were picked up from the streets and countryside of the British Isles and taken to the West Indies to be sold as slaves. Many of them no doubt ended up alongside black African slaves on the plantations. For about 200 years they were taken to Barbados where they were sold on the slave markets. Predating and overlapping the African slave trade.Faced with the prospect of being hanged only for being a Gypsy, many went into hiding. There is little doubt that amongst all those white slaves who were transported to Barbados were many many Gypsies from the British Isles. For Gypsies were classed as vagrants and were transported as slaves under the numerous Acts of Parliament during these years. For it was done, it was said at the time, "to free the kingdom of the burden of many strong and idle beggars, Egyptians, common and notorious thieves, and other dissolute and loose persons banished and stigmatized for gross crimes". Many Gipsies were banished from England, Wales, Scotland and Ireland, sometimes for merely being 'by habit and repute' Gipsies, is beyond dispute. Barbados was to become the West Indies capital of slavery, particularly Gypsy slavery and most of these were Gypsy Women. Though as well as Men slaves transported from Britain there were also many slave children transported there.A new decree was issued in Scotland in 1624 that travelling Gypsy men would be arrested and hanged, Gypsy women without children would be drowned, and Gypsy women with children would be whipped and branded on the cheek. There were also times then when the policy was only to send Gypsy women to the colonies, while the men were enslaved on galleys. Hundreds of thousands of Scots sold into slavery during Colonial America with white slavery to the American Colonies occurring as early as 1630 in Scotland. Then in 1655 the Cromwellian government ordered the arrest of all Egyptians in England and Scotland and their transportation or they could be forced into service for seven years without receiving any wage but giving them meat and clothes only for which the enslavers were to receive two scots shillings daily for each person during the first year and half that for the next. In 1656, Cromwell ordered that 2000 Irish children be taken to Jamaica and sold as slaves to English settlers. The English masters quickly began breeding the Irish women for both their own personal pleasure and for greater profit. Children of slaves were themselves slaves.

According to the Egerton manuscript, found in the British Museum and enacted in 1652: "it may be lawful for two or more justices of peace within any county, citty or towne, corporate belonging to the commonwealth to from tyme to tyme by warrant cause to be apprehended, seized on and detained all and every person or persons that shall be found begging and vagrant ... in any towne, parish or place to be conveyed into the Port of London, or unto any other port from where such person or persons may be shipped into a forraign collonie or plantation."

According to the Calendar of State Papers, Colonial Series, America and West Indies of 1701, we read of there being an estimated 25,000 slaves in Barbados, of whom 21,700 were white.

In 1661 'Commissions and Instructions' were issued anew to justices and constables, by Act of Parliament, with the view of arresting Gypsies. A great many Gypsies must have been deported to the British 'plantations' in Virginia, Jamaica and Barbados during the second half of the seventeenth century. That they had there to undergo a temporary, if not 'perpetual' servitude, seems very likely." (MacRitchie, 1894:102.Many gipsies were said [to be] subject from the age of eleven to thirty to the prostitution and lust of overseers, book-keepers, Negroes, &c., to be taken into keeping by gentlemen, who paid exorbitant hire for their use (Moreton, 1793:130) Gypsies came during colonial times, often forced by European Countries at religious & undesirable outcast, to move to the Colonies of America. Gypsies, according to the legal definition at that time in England, included "all such persons not being Felons wandering and pretending [i.e. identifying themselves to be Egyptians, or wandering in the Habite, Forme or Attyre] counterfayte Egyptians."

It was no doubt due to their roaming lifestyle that these Egyptians were more likely to be prosecuted and so to face a higher likelihood of transportation than others. Another fact was that a higher proportion of transported Gypsies were charged with horse stealing. Forced transportation of Gypsies into slavery began with their movement by slave ships to North America and the Caribbean. Of those persons who were transported during the late 1600s and early 1700s the main reason was due to vagrancy. Gypsies were of course seen as problems. At that time the European slave trade was at its peak with colonies in numerous parts of the so called New World with a constant demand for fresh slave labour. The African slave trade was just beginning during this same period.The judges of Edinburgh Scotland during the years 1662-1665 had ordered the enslavement and shipment to the colonies a large number of rogues and others who made life unpleasant for the British upper class. The Cromwellian government ordered the arrest of all Egyptians in England and Scotland and their transportation or they could be forced into service for seven years without receiving any wage but giving them meat and clothes only for which the enslavers were to receive two scots shillings daily for each person during the first year and half that for the next.

In 1665 at Edinburgh Scotland the Privy council gave warrants and power to George Hutchison, merchant, and his co partners to transport to Jamaica and Barbados Egyptians and other loose and dissolute persons. A reference dated November of that year, comments upon the motives for indenturing Gypsies and others in this way: The light regard paid to the personal right of individuals was shown by a wholesale deportation of poor people at this time to the West Indies out of a desire as well to promote the Scottish and English plantations in Jamaica and Barbados for the honour of their country, as to free the kingdom of the burden of many strong and idle beggars, Egyptians, common and notorious thieves, and other dissolute and loose persons banished and stigmatised for gross crimes (Chambers, 1858:304)..

Slave trading had expended by the 1700s when 10,000 people were being bought or kidnapped annually from the west African coast and taken to the Americas. It appears that Gypsies were tolerated when they were useful as farm labour, entertainers or blacksmiths, and were made to move on when no longer useful.Queen Anne issued an Act in 1713 "in which all persons pretending to be Gypsy or wandering in the habit or form of counterfeit gypsies Egyptians or pretending to have skills in physiognomy, palmistry or like crafty science or pretending to tell fortunes." The Act was further amended in 1716 and later by George1 by stating that such vagrants who had been convicted of no crimes could volunteer to be transported and some did.

Often for many Gypsies their only obvious escape from this was to change their name or identity or hide out in some remote area. Gipsies were also banished /deported from Britain to Australia and America in colonial times, for numerous crimes to undergo imprisonment in camps like Botany Bay. Often for merely being 'by habit and repute' Gipsies, is beyond dispute.

In 1714 British Merchants and Planters applied to the Privy Council for permission to ship them to the Caribbean was slaves. (MacRichie).

According to a document dated January 1st, 1715, 9 Scottish Border Gypsy Prisoners men and women... were sentenced to be transported to the plantations for being [by] habit and repute gipsies. Prisoners were sentenced to the West Indies – For being Gypsies. On the said gipsies coming here the town was brought under a burden [and] they had used endeavours with several merchants who have ships now going abroad [i.e., to transport them as slaves], for which they are to receive thirteen pounds sterling (Memorabilia,

1835:424-426). Roma formed part of the Atlantic Slave Trade then in the following year, according to a document dated January 1st, 1715, Prisoners were sentenced to be transported to the plantations for being [by] habit and repute gipsies.On the said gipsies coming here the town was brought under a burden [and] they had used endeavours with several merchants who have ships now going abroad [i.e., to transport them as slaves], for which they are to receive thirteen pounds sterling (Memorabilia, 1835:424-426). Among the family names of those individuals transported were Faa, Fenwick, Lindsey, Stirling, Robertson, Ross and Yorstoun all transported by the magistrate of Glasgow to the Virginia plantations. The most complete list of Gypsies sentenced to transportation appears in "Directory of Scots Banished to the American Plantations, 1650-1775", by David Dobson,1984,Baltimore, MD Genealogical Publishing Co. includes 16 Scottish Travellers forming 3 groups sentenced in 1682, 1715 and 1739. Gilbert Baillie, Gypsy, prisoner in Edinburgh, Tolbooth, transported from Greenock to N.Y., 21 Oct. 1682, ETRJohn Baillie, Gypsy, d.o. from Greenock to N.Y., same date. Robert Baillie, Gypsy and & thief, prisoner in Dumfries Tolbooth, 5-1-1739, banished to plantations in America for life. Jean Brown, Gypsy and thief, prisoner, as above. Mary & Peter Faa, Gypsies, prisoners in Jedburgh Tolbooth banished from there 30 Nov. 1714, transported via Glasgow on a Grennock ship…to Virginia Jean Hutson, Gypsy & thief, prisoner in Dumfries to America for life…1 May 1739.Mary Robertson, Gypsy, prisoner in Jedburgh, 9-1-1715 to Virginia. English surnames which frequently show up in various works on the Gypsies, include those of Bailey, Belcher, Boswell, Brown, Green, Hutson, Robinson, Robson, Roberts, Robertson, Smith, Stanley, and Sutherland, among others. The descendants of such early settlers would be justified in believing that their ancestors – who bore English and Scottish surnames and arrived on these shores in English ships – were indeed "English" or "Scottish." By the 1750s convicted slave prisoners on the Barbados island was offered freedom to leave but only if they were seen to have behaved. Another commentator Trigg recounted an episode when a group of Gypsies deported in the late 1700s were sent to Barbados. When they discovered their destination, both ship and Gypsies disappeared- to be absorbed into a Native American Indian nation.

In England in 1780 a group of Gypsies were hung in Northampton and their supporters threatened to set the town alight. Nothing is known about the crime for which the Gypsies committed and died or, indeed, if there was one. James Stanley was executed at Ilchester, for horse-stealing. Having received one respite for a week, it was expected he would have been reprieved, and the execution was delayed through the humanity of Mr. Hyatt, the Under-Sheriff, till six in the evening. Towards the last, he expressed great anxiety to be turned off, as all his own hopes of pardon had some time subsided. He was a Gypsy, and a great number of that fraternity attended, who took away the body in a very handsome coffin. James Squires who was originally convicted of stealing in 1785 and transported to penal institution in Australia as a convict in 1788. He was thought to be one of the first Gypsies who funded Australias first Brewery in 1798. His grandson James Farnell was to become the first native born Premier of New South Wales in 1877. The Parish officers in Pitcombe Somerset in 1792 charged members of the Cooper Gypsy family with the unlawful act of sleeping in the open air along with presuming to be Gypsies. Thomas Cooper pugalist boxer had been charged and convicted of highway robbery in Essex. He was not executed but transported to Van Diemans Land penal colony, later called Tasmania on *the Arab,* to arrive in Australia on 30th June 1834. Jack Cooper known as "fighting Jack" who was also transported. Along with Jacob Rewbray from St Margarets Westminster who was also charged at the Old Bailey with theft and was sentenced to penal transportation.

During that time many English Romanies Gypsies were owned by freed black slaves in Jamaica, Barbados, Cuba and Louisiana.The Romnichels or English Gypsies, began to come to the United States from England in 1850. Their arrival coincided with an increase in the demand for draft horses in agriculture and then in urbanization, and many Romnichels worked as horse-traders.

The earliest actual document known to us, dates from the time of the administration of Oliver Cromwell's successor, his son Richard.

When the first trans-Atlantic expulsion of Gypsies was instituted: as slaves to the southern plantations. In both Cuba and Louisiana today there are Afro -Romani populations resulting from intermarriage between freed African and Gypsy slaves. According to Ian Hancock The Roma Gypsies also arrived in the United States from Serbia, Russia and Austria-Hungary beginning in the 1880's, part of the larger wave of immigration from southern and eastern Europe in the late 19th and early 20th centuries. The arrival of Scottish Gypsy Travellers in North America also dates from about 1850, although the 18th-century transportation records appear to refer to this group. Unlike that of the other groups,Gypsies had been hung under "The Egyptian Act" for no more a reason than that of just being a Gypsy. Whilst their fatherless children were taken by the state as indentured apprentices by merchants and tradesmen and many were used as semi official slaves. Though as hangings were expensive the vast majority of convicted Gypsies were offered the alternative. That of being taken as slaves ships direct from Britain bound for the slave markets of the Americas, West Indies or the Australian penal colony. Often for no more a crime than damage to property. There are still iron notices on the Dorset county many stone bridges with the words "Anyone found damaging this bridge will be charged with felony and will be transported as slaves to Australia".

Gypsy white women were more likely to become slaves particularly for the Caribbean slave market for sexual relationships with the mainly black slaves which were essential for breeding purposes to obtain new generations of slaves for the sugar plantations. This was particularly so in the case of Barbados where young attractive full breasted white women were preferred to any others.A two shillings reward was offered for the capture of any such persons as being vagrants who were to be "whipped until his or her body was bloody put into the house of correction for hard labour, Any who did not give their place of birth, or who failed to work, were to be taken as apprentices or servants to her Majesties plantations or in any such British factory beyond the seas" for seven years. then returned to their homes. With the establishment of settlements in North America. A reprieve of the death sentence was offered should the condemned person consent to be transported to an American colony, and be entered into bond service i.e. slavery. Gypsy women were sent to work as spinners, boys in factories, men in mines and shipyards. Fourteen years later, they were freed by King Charles III.

CHAPTER FOUR

THE SLAVERY OF THE IRISH

In the early 1500s Henry VIII had declared himself to be 'King of Ireland' and granted several positions of Irish nobility to English settlers. He wanted to control Ireland from afar, and alter their customs and cultures to make them more English. The main stumbling block with this was his Protestant religion, with most of Ireland being Catholic. Henry used force to take control of large areas in Ireland. His invasion into Ireland was continued by his daughter, Queen Elizabeth I. British sailors begun capturing native Africans and selling them as slaves to New World settlers in the Americas. Towards the end of Elizabeth's 1st reign, Britain had defeated the Irish rebels at the Battle of Kinsale. This victory left more than 30,000 Irish soldiers as political prisoners. Britain brought in a policy of banishment. The Irish soldiers were forced to leave their country, with many moving to Spain and France to join foreign armies.Thousands of Irish rebels still remained in Ireland at that time until King James I's Proclamation in 1625 which ordered the Irish be placed in bondage. This required Irish political prisoners be sent overseas and sold to English settlers in the West Indies. This opened the door to the wholesale slavery of Irish men, women and children and ultimately they were transported, taken as prisoners to work as labourers. This was not indentured servitude but raw, brutal mistreatment that included many Irish being beaten to death.

During the reign of James 1st from 1603 -1625 the Irish were sold to the New World colonies America, the West Indies and south America whilst others were sold to Sweden in 1610. In 1618 a law allowed street children both Irish and English to be sent to Virginia. Street children taken from London's back alleys along with prostitutes, and poor migrants were searching for a brighter future and willing to sign up for indentured servitude. Their poor parents sought a better life for their offspring agreeing to send them, but most often, the children were sent despite their own protests and those of their families. The London authorities saw their actions more as an act of kindness or charity, and an opportunity for a poor child to better themselves as an apprentice in America, learn a trade, and avoid starvation at home. However tragically, once these unfortunate children arrived, half of them were dead within a year after being sold to farmers to work the fields. There was a continuous flow of white slaves imported to serve America's colonial masters in the New World during this time. Convicts were also persuaded to depart as a means to avoid lengthy sentences and executions on their home soil by entering a life of enslavement in the British colonies. The much maligned Irish were viewed as savages worthy of ethnic cleansing and despised for their rejection of Protestantism. These also made up a portion of America's first slave population, alongside others which included Quakers, Cavaliers, Puritans, Jesuits and Gypsy vagrants from England, Ireland, and Scotland throughout the years from 1618 to 1775.

Under the system of indenture, which was developed by the Virginia company, young men and women contracted themselves to work for a master for a period ranging from three to nine years. In return they were given passage to the colonies and subsistence during their tenure. Some were paid annual wages, but most were promised a one off payment at the end of their contract. – usually around 10 pounds or some land such as in Barbados where it was 10 acres.Oliver Cromwell himself oversaw the first wave of colonial transportation to the Caribbean. Writing to parliament after leading the slaughter at Drogheda in September 1649, the general reported that the 'officers were knocked on the head, and every tenth man of the soldiers killed, and the rest shipped for the Barbadoes'. Cromwell argued that massacre and transportation were benevolent forms of terrorism, as they would frighten the Irish into submission and thus 'prevent the effusion of blood for the future'.'My Day of Ruin Forever Until I Die'Some 30,000 indentured servants went to the Caribbean during these years with a similar figure going to North American colonies. Amongst those from Ireland were others throughout Britain These included dissenters and politically disaffected, but most consisted of members of the rural poor, suffering from the severe economic and social troubles in England at that time. Most were from the West country, East Anglia and Ireland. These were often tricked by merchants or middleman into selling their labour, or even kidnapped. Others sold themselves out of sheer desperation. But a large number saw it as an opportunity, particularly the young and those with energy and who saw immigration as a means to improve their circumstances for the better. Others saw it as a route to freedom of religion politics or economise. Few however knew just what they had actually let themselves in for. Indentured workers actually worked for far longer they should and were often sold on by their masters and were unable to negotiate their own contract and rarely bettered themselves at the end.The Irish had been forced from their land, kidnapped, fastened with heavy iron collars around their necks, chained to 50 other people and held in cargo holds aboard slave ships as they were transported to the American colonies. The British made it law that Irish political prisoners should be transported and sold to English settlers in America and the Caribbean. but there were not enough prisoners to keep up with the demand. To combat this, any minor infringement became punishable by transportation. Rogue gangs also roamed the streets of Ireland searching for potential kidnapping targets that could also be transported. Jordan and Walsh describe the Irish people at this time as "nothing more than human cattle". The white slave trade had continued to be very profitable during this time. English merchants were paid extremely well to take their white prisoners to the Americas and there they often exchanged them for tobacco which they then sold back in Britain on their return. Meanwhile the Irish slaves were toil in the tobacco fields of Virginia and Maryland and the sugar cane fields of Barbados and Jamaica. Ireland was to soon to become the English merchants biggest source of human livestock. England continued to ship tens of thousands of Irish slaves to slave plantations at the colonies for well over a century after. The Irish were to become the primary source of slave labour in the British American colonies.According to Forbes, the term "to Barbadoes" someone was synonymous with being kidnapped and deported to the Caribbean.

In the late 1640s and 1650s to be Barbadosed took on on the more modern meaning or term Shanghaied. Oliver Cromwell had "barbadosed" any Irish who refused to clear their land, and allowed for other Irish to be kidnapped from the streets of Ireland for shipment to Barbados as slaves. The British sold 330,000 Irish as slaves to the New World from 1641 to 1652. During this period Ireland's population fell from about 1,500,000 to 600,000 in one single decade. Whole Irish families were ripped apart, as the British did not allow Irish dads to take their wives and children with them across the Atlantic. This led to a helpless population of homeless women and children. Britain's solution was to auction them off as well. Any Irish resistance had been dealt with by transportation.

Jordan and Walsh believe that thousands of Irish people were transported over a hundred years, even for minor crimes. The journeys the prisoners took were highly dangerous for the Irish captives. Overcrowding and disease were major problems on the ships and life was cheap. The Irish prisoners were cheap to buy for the Caribbean settlers. A price of 900lbs of cotton was the standard amount paid. The African slaves though were a lot more expensive, averaging around three or four times that amount. This made the lives of Irish slaves less valuable to the landowners, and they suffered terrible cruelties because of this. Under the leadership of Oliver Cromwell, England invaded Scotland and won a stunning victory against the defending Scots at Dunbar in September 3, 1650.

This resulted in more prisoners than they knew what to do with (or could keep), and their cruel solution was to transport them to the colonies, to be sold as indentured servants.

'Man hunters' went around settlements on horseback with long whips forcing people, men, women and children, into holding pens outside the towns from which they were marched to the major ports, Kinsale, Bantry, or Galway. Where English slave ships picked them up at the ports.

During the 1650s, over 100,000 Irish children between the ages of 10 and 14 were taken from their parents and sold as slaves in the West Indies, Virginia and New England. In this decade, 52,000 Irish (mostly women and children) were sold to Barbados and Virginia alone. (more were sent to other islands in the West Indies) (A true and exact history of the Island of Barbados 1657).

Another 30,000 Irish men and women were also transported and sold to the highest bidder. The 'curse of Cromwell', a phrase is immortalised in a poem by William Butler Yeats. In the 1650s, the Kerryman Éamonn an Dúna entitled 'My Day of Ruin Forever Until I Die', the forced removal of Catholics to Connacht with their forced labour in American colonies. Mixing English and Irish in his verse, an Dúna wrote that if the English did not 'shoot … kill … strip … tear … hack … [or] hang …' Tories, rebels and priests, they would ship them to the colonies 'chum tobac do dhéanamh' [to make tobacco grow] … Transport, transplant, mo mheabhair ar Bhéarla [that's my memory/understanding of English]'. While the English construed Irish colonisation as the work of God, an Dúna recognised it as a curse. Persecuted Catholics from Ireland worked on the plantations. Though none of these ever made it back to their homeland to tell of their suffering. a leading role in the settlement of Jamaica and the Carolinas. Leading to the Third English Civil War, Parliament declared war on Scotland shortly after Scotland proclaimed Charles II King of Great Britain, France and Ireland. To sell the Irish as slaves was seen as natural by the English of the time. The prevailing attitude was that an Irish Catholic was less than human. To kill them was a heroic act, profiting from Irish White slavery was seen almost as a humanitarian act. Anyone who was considered to be a'vagrant' or vagabond (in other words homeless) such as a Gypsy or an enemy of the new regime such as the entire Catholic clergy and anyone who was young enough to be useful for slave labour, was transported.

It is estimated that transportation to Barbados was the fate of 50,000 Irish people between the years of 1652 and 1656. The practice had become so popular, one resident wrote, that people had started to"make a verb of it, to Barbados you".

The Irish slaves were next in line to black slaves when it came to being exposed to cruel treatment. The Irish were considered rebellious. Plantation owners used extreme violence to ensure obedience. Many ended up in Barbados working the sugar fields, where they had an acute need for as many labourers as they could get.By the mid 1600s the Irish were forced into a form of slavery, though one far less severe and less consequential than which Africans endured for close to 400 years in the Americas. William Petty research in Ireland and his wider knowledge of the Atlantic economy led him to conclude that, rather than destroying the Irish, English interests would be best served in the colonies by enslaving them like 'negroes':'You value the people who have been destroyed in Ireland as slaves and negroes are usually rated, viz, at about 15 one with another; men being sold for 25, children for 5. Why should not insolvent thieves be punished with slavery rather than death. So as being slaves they may be forced to as much labour, and as cheap fare, as nature will endure, and thereby become as two men added to the commonwealth, and not as one taken away from it.'Petty's account proves that some very powerful members of the Cromwellian regime envisioned enslaving Irish and 'negros' in parallel fashion. Significantly, in the British Caribbean, white servants made up the majority of the unfree plantation workforce. Irish sailors voyaging to the West Indies on commercial ventures or with Prince Rupert's Royalist fleet in 1652 would have seen Irish people subjected to plantation bondage. Irish servants and others from England and Scotland referred to themselves as 'slaves'. African slaves also regarded Irish field hands as slaves. In 1655, Irish sailors had themselves been transported after being captured serving with Royalist forces. Their peers petitioned the Commonwealth to release those it had 'most barbarously ... sold and sent away ... for slaves into some foreign plantations'. An anonymous writer on Barbados, most probably Major John Scott, wrote in 1667 that the Irish were 'derided by the Negroes, and branded with the epithet of "white slaves"'.

Africans referred to the Irish as slaves, as the Irish did themselves, to reflect the brutal exploitation they endured as unfree plantation workers who, having been kidnapped or transported, were violently forced to work against their will. Baily referred to himself as a 'bond-slave', a biblical term for a slave not held to lifelong bondage. Historians have been wrong in assessing such references as borrowings from seventeenth-century political speech, where 'slavery' described the condition of those living under tyrannical governments. Instead, in the accounts above, the slavery referred to was economic, different from the lifelong enslavement of Africans but a form of slavery nonetheless. Unfree whites who called themselves slaves or were called such by black slaves were known in law as 'indentured servants'. Irish field hands called themselves slaves because they were the term-bound, chattel property of the planters who purchased them. They were itemised as the 'goods and chattels' of their masters on contracts and in estate inventories—often beside 'negroes', livestock, hardware and other household goods. Like 'negroe' slaves, they could be sold again and again without their consent. Historians have often argued that 'servants' weren't bought and sold, only their contracts were. This is a legal fiction, not a material reality. Contracts did not cut sugar cane and weed tobacco fields; chattel workers did. Contracts, which kidnapped and transported people without their agreement, did not prevent enslavement. Instead, contracts led to enslavement, transforming people into term-bound chattel property. Contracts commodified more than 'servant' labour; they commodified the person as a species of capital collateral.

Planters used 'servants', like slaves, as financial instruments to escape bankruptcy, to satisfy creditors, to liquidate estates, and to resolve debts and broken contracts..

The political 'slavery' of English colonialism led to the economic enslavement of the Irish on colonial plantations. Their plight is part of Ireland's tragic colonial history Racial slavery and the chattel, term bondage imposed on the Irish and other Europeans were crucial innovations in the early history of capitalism, a history where the plantation complex took centre stage. After Oliver Cromwell had gained his decisive victory against Charles II at Worcester, he once again had more prisoners than he could cope with. As his success proved with the transportation of the Dunbar prisoners (not so much for the Scottish prisoners!) So it was Parliament approved the same solution to the prisoners from Worcester. So it was that many were shipped to the Saugus Iron Works in Massachusetts, but at least some 8000 Englishmen prisoners were shipped to Barbados to be indentured to plantation owners there and again with a huge purse for Cromwell.

Cromwell found that by transporting his royalist prisoners of war to the colonies supposedly as servants. He had found a way to rid himself of future potential enemies. Whilst making a profit at the same time. Some of the Irish men were allowed to take their families with them but only to find they were all separated on arrival at Barbados which was the main stopping place where they were sold, one account tells us, the husband in one place, the wife another, and the children in another place, so as not to receive any solace from one another. After Cromwell victories at Drigheda, Worcester and Dundbar in 1649-1651, meant there was an influx of Irish and Scots to the colonies, Cromwell wrote afterwards, that when they submitted these officers were knocked on the head, and every tenth man of the soldiers were killed, and the rest shipped to Barbados. These Irish were troublesome on the island and the planters pleased with him to send no more. Between the years 1659 and 1663, during the Cromwellian conquest of Ireland under the command of Oliver Cromwell, thousands of Irish Catholics were forced into servitude. Cromwell had an acute hatred of the Catholic religion, and those many Irish Catholics who had participated in Confederate Ireland. He confiscated their land and transported them to the West Indies as indentured servants, along with Scottish Highlanders and other Scotsmen. These were all forcibly taken and transported abroad at this time. It is also on record that a considerable number of Highland Jacobite supporters, who had been captured in the aftermath of Culloden and subsequently the rigorous Government sweeps of the Highlands to root out Jacobite fugitives and transgressors of the new laws against Highland culture itself, languished in fetid prison hulks on the River Thames for months, until sentenced to transportation to the Carolinas as indentured servants/slaves.

Even if an Irish woman somehow obtained her freedom, her kids would remain slaves of her master. Thus, Irish mothers, even with this new found emancipation, would seldom abandon their kids and would remain in servitude. Girls as young as 12 were taken advantage of by their masters or sold to increase their market share: They bred the Irish women and girls with African men to produce slaves with a distinct complexion. These new "mulatto" slaves brought a higher price than Irish livestock and, likewise, enabled the settlers to save money rather than purchase new African slaves. This practice of interbreeding Irish females with African men carried on for many years and was widespread by 1681 when legislation was introduces "forbidding the practice of mating Irish slave women to African slave men for the purpose of producing slaves for sale." It was however only stopped as it interfered with the slavers transporters profits.In the mid 1600s, the Irish were the main slaves sold to Antigua and Montserrat. Some historians today are of the belief that this was not indentured servitude but raw, brutal mistreatment that included being beaten to death. That not only were the Irish forced from their land. But that they were kidnapped, fastened with heavy iron collars around their necks, chained to 50 other people and held in cargo holds aboard ships as they were transported to the American colonies. During the early colonial period, free European and free African settlers socialized and married. Intermarriages existed in the colonies for over a hundred years until the birth and evolution of white racism. The Irish and African slaves were housed together and were forced to mate to provide the plantation owners with the additional slaves they needed.

Jordan and Walsh also highlight another horrific act that took place on these new settlements. The settlers would breed with the female workers, to produce more cheap labour. The child would be under the ownership of the settlers, and the mothers would rarely leave their children in such conditions, even after their terms of labour had expired. Another method settlers used to produce cheap labour was to breed the Irish women with the African men. The resulting skin tone of the offspring was more valuable to landowners in the slave markets. This practice was made illegal in 1681 in Ireland, the Jacobite Wars ended in 1691 with William of Orange finally defeating James II's armies leaving thousands of Irish Catholics unwilling to accept the rule of the Protestants.In 1723 Fr Cornelius Nary estimated that 'fifteen thousand to twenty thousand souls' had been transported into 'slavery'.

In Ireland under English rule (1903), Thomas Addis Emmet, the American grandson of the United Irishman of the same name, claimed that 120,000–130,000 were shipped to the colonies. Michael Davitt recorded that 'all the Irish who could not be shipped off to England's colonies in America and the West Indies as slaves were hunted remorselessly into Connaught'. James Connolly wrote in The re-conquest of Ireland (1915) that 'over 100,000 men, women and children were transported to the West Indies, there to be sold into slavery upon the tobacco plantations'.These Irish prisoners were given the opportunity to leave the country for France. Around 30,000 Irish people took this opportunity and they became known as the Wild Geese. Most of those that refused were transported to labour camps. The United Irishmen's unsuccessful 1798 Rebellion created the opportunity for the British to ship thousands more Irishmen and women overseas, including Australia. The sequence finally ended in 1839, when Britain finally decided to end their involvement in the slave trade. Records show that, after the 1798 Irish Rebellion, thousands of Irish slaves were sold to both America and Australia. There were horrible abuses of Irish captives. One British ship threw 1,302 slaves overboard into the Atlantic Ocean so that the crew would have plenty of food to eat. Many people today will avoid calling these people slaves, preferring "Indentured Servants", to describe those Irish deportation into slavery. However, in most cases from the 1600 and 1700s, Irish slaves were nothing more than human cattle. If a planter whipped or branded or beat an Irish slave to death, it was never a crime. A death was a monetary setback, but far cheaper than killing a more expensive African. In Barbados today there are still some descendants of those Irish vagrants that were captured and sold as slaves. They are called the Red Legs, a poverty stricken group of the population. Apparently they owe their strange name name to sun burnt legs emerging from their kilts when stepping off the slave boats.

As well as the Irish, Oliver Cromwell was also responsible for sending thousands of Scots to slavery in the Caribbean, with prisoners from the Jacobite Uprisings, with all of them facing the same fate. In the 1630s large numbers of Scottish people, possibly as many as 100,000, were said to be rounded up and transported to the West Indies and American colonies to be sold into slavery. In addition to this practice, political prisoners were routinely sold into slavery along with Gypsies. According to the Egerton manuscript in the British Museum and enacted in 1652: "it may be lawful for two or more justices of peace within any county, city or town, corporate belonging to the commonwealth to from time to time by warrant cause to be apprehended, seized on and detained all and every person or persons that shall be found begging and vagrant... in any town, parish or place to be conveyed into the Port of London, or unto any other port from where such person or persons may be shipped into a foreign colony or plantation." According to the Calendar of State Papers, Colonial Series, America and West Indies of 1701. Of an estimated 25,000 slaves in Barbados, 21,700 were white. Affluent and powerful local government officials, who likely had a stake in the plantations, slave trade and the associated benefits, were happy to oblige in this practice. Whilst rich English merchants who had previously made their fortunes as planters in Barbados and who were now living in luxury on their fine estates in England were also known to have put in special requests to the city council for young well breasted Barbados women slaves. With the result being that many were shipped to them to meet their personal sexual favours.

CHAPTER FIVE

THE SALEE ROVERS
BARBARY CORSAIR PIRATES

Pirates day

The pirate ship was anchored in the bay
all the lonesome sea sick sailors
were many miles away
the harbour lights were fading
the moon came into view
all the mermaids were all singing
it was a typical crazy night in Poole

The pubs were all shut and boarded
there was no ale left in the vaults
the fishes were all swimming
deep out at sea a float
there were still stories in the docklands
written down in history

The pirate crew were merry
just awoke from their sleep
there were flags of skull and crossbones
the police all took a peep

The coastguards were alerted
they'd stowed the ale away
hidden it in secret caves

49

down at Lulworth bay

The writer told his stories
Robert Louis Stevenson was his name
he wrote of treasure island
he lived at Westbournes main

They say that Enid Blyton
lived in Swanage town
she based her tales on Noddy
Corfe castle and Poole town
the land was owned by Talbot
given by the crown

Gulliver the pirate
sailed for botany bay
he contraband tea
so many miles away
they still fly the jolly roger
at Poole speedway today

You can still see the lord Nelson singing
if you look across from Poole bay
for the waves still rise at stud-land
where all the nudists have their day
its all just local history
passed on down in Poole today

Ray Wills

On the Caribbean Coast

On the Caribbean coastline
they took the sad old souls
all the maids of innocence
they wore their precious gowns of old
along with the gentlemen of virtue
the sultry Gypsy wenches
On the Caribbean Coast

On the Caribbean coastline
they took the sad old souls
all the maids of innocence
they wore their precious gowns of old
along with the gentlemen of virtue
the sultry Gypsy wenches
and the whores of London town

The Barbary pirates corsairs and the like
the slaves were deep within the galleys
their bodies set in sweat and lice
their tears they shed for everyone
both the living and the dead
for the futures for their birthright
afore they all were wed

The cock it crowd at daybreak
come see the natives naked breasts
the Jamaican sun was scorching hot
for the ships upon the waves
the slaves deep below the decks

tomorrow offered salvation
to the wise man and the fools
to all those who sailed the ships of life
before their golden honeymoon

All the richest merchants
and planters yet to be
set sail at dawn as day broke
for to sail the seven seas
they plundered and they took all of the best
all that their monies could buy
when the slavery trade offered liberty
with all the riches yet to be

The cannons roared at twilight
and the captives all were set free
to live a life of freedom
like pirate slaves upon the seven seas

Ray Wills

System Templars Tabernacles and Fools

He was put there by popular choice
he was a man of the people
with the theme and the voice
his was the reason
they were slaves and all walked in line
all the wise and the free
midst the rhymes and the vines

The congress man idioms
all those men of the plains
that old schoolboy rhetoric
and their forgotten cultured names

His was the vision
and the last freedoms call
when the hands that were shackled
were lost in the fall

All the masters with their doctrines
all the worldly and wise
the fine schools where they were taught
where their plans were surmised

The funny handshakes
with their false flags a few
and the sayings they spouted
on the rivers of lies
when the truth it was out
but their hands they were tied

Oh the masters of wars
with their doctrines of peace
in their temples of grace
where the crooked tongues preached

Where the bible was held
in such high revelry
but they read it with a smile
for it was all just a ruse and a tease
to control you and me.

Ray Wills

CAPT CROKER HORROR STRICKEN AT ALGIERS,
on witnessing the Miseries of the Christian Slaves chaind & in Irons driven home after labour by Infidels with large Whips. Page ibid

Our understanding of Pirates today conjures up childhood memories and images of swashbuckling outlaws of the oceans. As depicted in the literary works of Robert Louis Stevensons Treasures Island. Such as the pirates Long John Silver and Blackbeard or even in the exploits of the legendry Captain Hook. However these Corsair Barbary pirates were not of this fantasy. These pirates were authorised by governments and manned large fleets of ships full of sailors who raided European and American ships and took as slaves their captives or raided coastal villages and took fishermen or common village peoples as slaves. They consisted of Turks and commercial privateers and occasionally Europeans who had converted to Islam. By late 1500s there were probably around 500 British slaves in Algiers. During the late 1500s and early 1600s, around 35,000 White European Christian slaves were held throughout this time on the Barbary Coast. Of these, the Barbary corsairs, may have enslaved as many as 25,000 Britons. They were seized every year to work as galley slaves, labourers and concubines for Muslim overlords in what is today Morocco, Tunisia, Algeria and Libya. These British men, women and children taken as slaves endured miserable conditions –

invariably with little prospect of ever seeing their homes again. The Royal Navy's inability to protect British citizens indicates its weakness at the time. The corsairs captured and enslaved more than a million Europeans between 1530 and 1780 in a series of raids that depopulated coastal towns from Sicily to Cornwall in England. The cost of the goods they stole and destroyed was enormous. A large proportion of those taken captive – and of the treasure seized was British. With the help of Dutch and British renegades, the corsairs had learned to sail and navigate square-rigged ships – that the corsairs focused their attacks on the people of northern Europe. They maintained order on the ships which took foreign merchandise and enslaved their crews. They were paid most generously and despite the laws of their Muslim faith they were allowed alcohol, tobacco and opium. They enslaved prisoners taken in war. Most of those taken were sailors, taken with their ships, but a good many were fishermen and coastal villagers.

Not content with attacking ships and sailors, the corsairs also sometimes raided coastal settlements, generally running their craft onto unguarded beaches, and creeping up on villages in the dark to snatch their victims and retreat before the alarm could be sounded.

They practically depopulated parts of the Italian coast. Italy being the most popular target. "One of the things that both the public and many scholars have tended to take as given is that slavery was always racial in nature – that only blacks have been slaves. But that is not true. The Ottoman provinces in North Africa were nominally under Ottoman soverginty, but in reality they were mostly autonomous. They prowled the coasts of Spain and southern Italy and the great islands – Majora, Minorca, Sarduina and Sicily started to live in fear of these corsairs. Their sweeps were sudden, unpredictable and terrifying, the damage immense. "From bases on the Barbary coast, North Africa, the Barbary Pirates raided ships travelling through the Mediterranean and along the northern and western coasts of Africa, plundering their cargo and enslaving the people they captured. They conducted raids along seaside towns of Italy, Spain, France, England, the Netherlands and as far away as Iceland, capturing men, women and children. On some occasions, settlements such as Baltimore, Ireland were abandoned following the raid, only being resettled many years later. During the 16th and 17th centuries more slaves were taken south across the Mediterranean than west across the Atlantic. Some were ransomed back to their families, some were put to hard labour in north Africa, and the unluckiest worked themselves to death as galley slaves.

The Calendar of State Papers Domestic for the reign of Charles I (CSPD, a collection of papers of the secretaries of state that are a rich source of contemporary detail), records that, in May 1626, a certain Hugh Ross "drinks to the Duke [of Buckingham's] health, and wishes all his enemies in Algiers to relieve 3,000 English who are there, and 1,500 English who are in Sallee in misery. Two brothers who were prominent within their corsair pirate ranks as leaders were Oruch and Hizir, whom the Christians were to refer to as Barbarossa -the red beards. They were adventurers from the eastern Mediterranean born on the island of Lesbos which was situated between Islam and Christendom territories and spanned both worlds. Their father was an Ottoman cavalryman their mother a Greek Christian. Their commitment to Islam and then their piracy had been shaped by the Christian order of the Knights of St John. Oruch had been taken into captivity by the Knights who were themselves ruthless slavers. They could be unscrupulous as any corsair. Oruch was a shackled slave for two years at their Rhodes settlement then he endured a terrible life as an oarsman in their galleys before escaping by filing his chains and swimming away to freedom. It was this experience which was to shape his future as both an Islamic warrior and a corsair pirate leader. The brothers first appeared around 1512 as adventurers with nothing to lose. They were both skilled at navigation and seamanship. In one month alone Hazir claimed to have taken twenty one merchant ships and 3,800 men, women and children. As the fame and notoriety of this one leader so did the leg ends, Whilst Oruch, short, stocky, powerful, given to explosions of rage, with a gold ring in his right ear and his red beard and hair, was a figure of inspiration and dread. To the oral history and poems of the Muslims of Spain s oceans and beyond he was seen as an Islamic Robin Hood. With the talismanic powers of a sorcerer, he was seen as if God had made him invulnerable to sword thrusts, that he had signed a pact with the devil to make his corsair ships invisible to their eyes. So it was that these myths were spread abroad.By the late 1520s there were at least forty corsair captains on the Barbary coasts under the leadership of Hayrettin all deployed to harry the Christian sea. He projected himself as an awesome presence, invincible, frightening, brilliant. He projected himself as the manifestation of the will of God and the imperial authority of Suleiman which allowed him to escape ambushes, dodge storms and capture cities. He came in his own words amongst the Christian fleets like the sun among the stars at whose appearance their light vanished. His knowledge of the oceans was unmatched. Over a ten year period he took 10,000 people from the coasts lines of Barcelona and Valencia alone. He became known simply as Barbarossa and the subject of many stories and songs. The corsairs who followed him gave him 12 per cent of their takings.The corsairs came from many parts of the world many were even renegade Christians. The corsairs gave their many ships vivid beautiful names such as *The Pearl, The Door of Neptune, The Sun, the Golden Lemon Tree, The Rose of Algiers*, etc.

They ransacked Vieste in southern Italy in 1554 where they took 6,000 captives. The Algerians took 7,000 slaves in the Bay of Naples in 1544, in a raid that drove the price of slaves so low it was said you could "swap a Christian for an onion." Spain, too, suffered large-scale attacks. A raid on Granada in 1566 netted 4,000 men, women, and children, it was said to be "raining Christians in Algiers." For every large-scale raid of this kind there would have been dozens of smaller ones. In 1566, a party of 6,000 Turks and Corsairs sailed up the Adriatic and landed at Fracaville. The Turks took control of over 500 square miles of abandoned villages all the way to Serracapriola.

In 1575, Cervantes was returning from Naples—after serving for six years in the regiment of Figueroa, and losing the use of his left arm at Lepanto—to revisit his own country; when his ship El Sol was attacked by several Corsair galleys commanded by Arnaut Memi; and, after a desperate resistance, in which Cervantes took a prominent part, was forced to strike her colours. Cervantes thus became the captive of a renegade Greek, one Deli Memi, a Corsair reïs, who, finding upon him letters of recommendation from persons of the highest consequence, Don John of Austria among them, concluded that he was a prisoner of rank, for whom a heavy ransom might be asked. Accordingly the future author of Don Quixote was loaded with chains and harshly treated, to make him the more anxious to be ransomed. The ransom, however, was slow in coming, and meanwhile the captive made several daring, ingenious, but unsuccessful attempts to escape, with the natural consequences or stricter watch and greater severities. At last, in the second year of his captivity, he was able to let his friends know of his condition; whereupon his father strained every resource to send a sufficient sum to release Miguel, and his brother Rodrigo, who was in the like plight. The brother was set free, but Cervantes himself was considered too valuable for the price.

With the help of his liberated brother he once more concerted a plan of escape. In a cavern six miles from Algiers, where he had a friend, he concealed by degrees forty or fifty fugitives, chiefly Spanish gentlemen, and contrived to supply them with food for six months, without arousing suspicion. It was arranged that a Spanish ship should be sent by his brother to take off the dwellers in the cave, whom Cervantes now joined. The ship arrived; communications were already opened; when some fishermen gave the alarm; the vessel was obliged to put to sea; and, meanwhile, the treachery of one of the captives had revealed the whole plot to Hasan Pasha, the Viceroy, who immediately sent a party of soldiers to the cavern. Cervantes, with his natural chivalry, at once came to the front and took the whole blame upon himself. Surprised at this magnanimity, the Viceroy—who is described in Don Quixote as "the homicide of all human kind"—sent for him, and found him as good as his word. No threats of torture or death could extort from him a syllable which could implicate any one of his fellow-captives. His undaunted manner evidently overawed the Viceroy, for instead of chastizing he purchased Cervantes from his master for five hundred gold crowns.

Nothing could deter this valiant spirit from his designs upon freedom. Attempt after attempt had failed, and still he tried again. Once he was very near liberty, when a Dominican monk betrayed him; even then he might have escaped, if he would have consented to desert his companions in the plot: but he was Cervantes. He was within an ace of execution, thanks to his own chivalry, and was kept for five months in the Moor's bagnio, under strict watch, though without blows—no one ever struck him during the whole of his captivity, though he often stood in expectation of impalement or some such horrible death. At last, in 1580, just as he was being taken off, laden with chains, to Constantinople, whither Hasan Pasha had been recalled, Father Juan Gil effected his ransom for about £100 of English money of the time, and Miguel de Cervantes, after five years of captivity, was once more free. As has been well said, if Don Quixote and all else of his had never been written, "the proofs we have here of his greatness of soul, constancy, and cheerfulness, under the severest of trials which a man could endure, would be sufficient to ensure him lasting fame."

In the first half of the 1600s, these Barbary corsairs- pirates from the Barbary Coast of North Africa were authorised by their governments to attack the shipping of Christian countries- ranged all around Britain's shores. In their lantern-rigged xebecs (a type of ship) and oared galleys, they grabbed ships and sailors, and sold the sailors into slavery.Admiralty records show that during this time the corsairs plundered British shipping pretty much at will, taking no fewer than 466 vessels between 1609 and 1616, and for over 300 years, the coastlines of the south west of England were plundered by Barbary pirates (corsairs).On 12th of August the Mayor of Plymouth writes that there are general fears for the ships from Virginia and Newfoundland. Twenty seven ships and 200 persons had been take by Turkish pirates in ten days. (Calendar of State Papers 1860) Mayor of Poole Dorset to the Privy council stated that, Unless measures are taken, the Newfoundland fleet of 250 sail, having on board four or five thousand men of the western parts, will be surprised by the Turkish pirates.(Calendar of State Papers. 1860)

In July of 1625 the Barbary Corsairs who were better known in England as the Salee Rovers captured Lundy Island in the British channel as their fortified naval base. From which they attacked the unprotected villages of northern Cornwall. Then in 1631 they had set their eyes on the richly populated coasts of southern Ireland and set sail with a force of some 200 Islamic soldiers to the village of Baltimore.

An entry in the Calendar of State Papers in May 1625 stated, 'The Turks are upon our coasts. They take ships only to take the men to make slaves of them. Corsairs were said to have captured 1,000 seamen in the Plymouth area alone. On the 12th of August the Mayor of Plymouth wrote to the Privy council in London pleading for naval assistance because in just 10 days some 27 ships were taken. Along with all their crews of some 200 men, all of whom were now slaves (Dalrymple,2004). A CSPD entry for 12 August that year reads: "The pirates are 26 or 27 sail strong. Sir Francis Stewart sent out five ships against them, but they are far better sailors than the English ships. Corsairs were said to have captured 1,000 seamen in the Plymouth area alone. From the chalky cliffs of England they penetrated the straights of Dover and St Georges channel. Even to the western shores of Ireland.

Almost all the inhabitants of the village of Baltimore, in Ireland, were captured by corsairs in 1631. Baltimore is a small Irish village a local fisherman captured by the pirates did a deal with them to save his life. He led them to a sleepy village where they took prisoners of 89 women and children plus 20 men were captured by the pirates. After they endured a journey of 38 days they arrived in Algiers where they were sold as slaves. The children were separated from their parents. The women were n the main employed as sew mistresses or became concubines. Whilst the men were taken as galley slaves if they were lucky.. In England King Charles Ist was asked to intervene to secure their freedoms but he declined On the grounds that it would only encourage more such outrages in the future. Only 3 of the women ever made it back to their own country. Following the attack the remaining villagers moved to a nearby larger settlement further away from the coast and Baltimore became a desolate place. There were other raids in England including Devon and Cornwall. A raiding party arrived at Mounts bay in Cornwall in August of that year raided Mount's Bay capturing 60 men, women and children and taking them into slavery. Unlike their victims, corsair vessels had two means of propulsion: galley slaves as well as sails. This meant they could row up to any becalmed sailing ship and attack at will. They carried many different flags, so when they were under sail they could run up whatever ensign was most likely to gull a target. US historian Robert Davis stated that Scholars have long known of the slave raids on Europe. calculated that the total number captured- although small compared with the 12 million Africans shipped to the Americas in later years- was far higher than previously recognised. Robert Davis concluded that 1 million to 1.3 million ended up in bondage. All unsuspecting inhabitants were swept into such cruel captivity and slavery. Whilst St Keverne was also repeatedly attacked, and boats out of Looe, Penzance, Mouse hole and other Cornish ports were boarded, their crews taken captive and the empty ships left to drift.

At the time Sir John Eliot, Vice Admiral of Devon, declared that the seas around England "seemed theirs. The villagers saw the ships at anchor and they fled for their lives to the nearby church, but they were caught. Altogether the slavers took 60 people onto their ships. They all set sail and eventually arrived at the slave markets of North Africa.

King Charles 1 sent a mission to north Africa in an attempt to buy back 2000 British slaves. Many such ransoms were paid regularly to the Turks by families and groups to free their family members throughout the 17th century.One spectacular raid by the corsairs at Iceland in 1627 took nearly 400 captives. Of these there were only 70 survivors eight years later. For as well as malnutrition, overcrowding, overwork, and brutal punishment, slaves faced epidemics of plague, which usually wiped out 20 to 30 percent of the white slaves.

Many of the ships sailing to America and the Caribbean travelled from Bristol and passed within view of the island of Lundy. It was simply a question of the pirates following them until they were out of sight of land and then attacking. Throughout these years the pirates operated freely in British waters, even sailing up the Thames estuary to pick off prizes and raid coastal towns. The situation was so bad that in December 1640 a Committee for Algiers was set up by Parliament to oversee the ransoming of captives. At that time it was reported that there were some 3,000 to 5,000 English people in captivity in Algiers. Although by the mid-1600s the British themselves were running a brisk trans-Atlantic trade in blacks, although many British crewmen themselves became the property of Arab corair pirate raiders. Charities were also set up to help ransom the captives and local fishing communities all raise money to liberate their own. A priest negotiates ransom for the release of slaves Europeans sometimes attempted to buy their people out of slavery, but no real system emerged before around 1640. Then the attempts became more systematic and were sometimes state subsidised, as in Spain and France. Almost all the actual work, however- from collecting the funds, to voyaging to Barbary, to negotiating with the slave owners there - was carried out by clergy, mostly members of the Trinitarian or Mercedarian orders.Emanuel d'Aranda, a Flemish soldier who was himself enslaved in Algiers in 1640–42, not only paints a portrait of men abandoned, destitute and unvalued but also one in which Britons were the most unfortunate of the unfortunate. "All nations made some shift to live, save only the British. The winter I was in the slave bagnio, I observed there died above 20 of them out of pure want. Nor are they therefore much esteemed by the Turks; for a British man is sold at 60 or 70 Patacoons [the local currency], when a Spaniard or Italian is valued at 150, or 200."

The corsair Pirates returned many times to pillage the same territory. in less than a 10-year period: 700 were captured in a single raid in 1636, 1,000 in 1639 and 4,000 in 1644.The pirates set up semi-permanent bases on the islands of Ischia and Procida, practically within the mouth of the Bay of Naples, from which they took their pick of commercial traffic. From which they plundered British ships.

Thousands of Dutch, Germans and British 'languished for years in the chains of Barbary,' without the aid of organised clergy or state funds for their release. "The pirates plundered British shipping pretty much at will". So wrote the Reverend Devereux Spratt- carried off in April 1641 for several years' bondage in Algiers, while attempting a simple voyage across the Irish Sea from County

Cork to England. Spratt's experience has been largely forgotten now, though it was far from unique in his day.

In 1645 Barbary pirates on the Cornish coast kidnapped 240 men, women and children. Then in 1646 Parliaments Edmund Cason went to Algiers and negotiated their ransoms and release paying around £30 per man (women were more expensive to ransom) and arranged for freedom before he ran out of money.

The large-scale Ransoming like the one headed by Edmund Casson were rare, with the result that Protestant Britons were often more demoralised and likely to die in captivity than European Catholics. Casson spent the last 8 years of his life trying to arrange the release of a further 400 slaves from captivity.

Whilst England set aside its 'Algerian Duty' from customs income to finance redemptions, but much of this was diverted to other uses. One ex-slave noted at the time: "All of the nations made some shift to live, save only the English, who it seems are not so shift-full as others, and have no great kindness one for another. The winter I was in [captivity], I observed there died above twenty of them out of pure want." "When we had arrived [in Cork], I made a request to Lord Inchaquoin to give me a passport for England. I took boat to Youghal and then embarked on the vessel *John Filmer*, which set sail with 120 passengers. `But before we had lost sight of land, we were captured by Algerine pirates, who put all the men in irons".By the mid 1600s Europe itself was starting to be on the receiving end of the slavery trade which they had only just inflicted on West Africa. Though the numbers they slaved to Islam far exceeded those of the black slaves taken by them earlier in the 1500s and where Atlantic slaving was a matter of cold business, in the Mediterranean it was heightened by mutual religious hatred. The Islamic raiding was designed to both damage the material infrastructure of Spain and Italy and to undermine the spiritual and physic basis of the opponents lives.

Samuel Pepys mentions the Barbary slave trade in his diary, in an entry from 8th February 1661 he wrote- "I went to the Fleece Tavern to drink; and there we spent till four o'clock, telling stories of Algiers, and the manner of the life of slaves there! And truly Captain. Mootham and Mr. Dawes (who have been both slaves there) did make me fully acquainted with their condition there: as, how they eat nothing but bread and water. How they are beat upon the soles of their feet and bellies at the liberty of their padron. How they are all, at night, called into their master's Bagnard; and there they lie. How the poorest men do use their slaves best. How some rogues do live well, if they do invent to bring their masters in so much a week by their industry or theft; and then they are put to no other work".

The slavery system was not, however, entirely without humanity. Slaves usually got Fridays off. Likewise, when bagno men were in port, they had an hour or two of free time every day between the end of work and before the bagno doors were locked at night. During this time, slaves could work for pay, but they could not keep all the money they made. Even bagno slaves were assessed a fee for their filthy lodgings and rancid food. Public slaves also contributed to a fund to support bagno priests. This was a strongly religious era, and even under the most horrible conditions, men wanted a chance to say confession and — most important — receive extreme unction. There was almost always a captive priest or two in the bagno, but in order to keep him available for religious duties, other slaves had to chip in and buy his time from the pasha. Some galley slaves thus had nothing left over to spend on food or clothing, though in some periods, free Europeans living in the cities of Barbary contributed to the upkeep of bagno priests. While Barbary corsairs looted the cargo of ships they captured, their primary goal was to capture non-Muslim people for sale as slaves or for ransom. Those who had family or friends who might ransom them were held captive, the most famous of these was the author Miguel de Cervantes, who was held for almost five years.

Others were sold into various types of servitude. Captives who converted to Islam were generally freed, since enslavement of Muslims was prohibited; but this meant that they could never return to their native countries. They took people in the middle of the night whilst "peaceful and still naked in their beds." Women were easier to catch than men, and coastal areas could quickly lose their entire child-bearing population. Fishermen were afraid to go out, or would sail only in convoys. Eventually, Italians gave up much of their coast.

In 1675 Sir John Narborough, backed by a Royal Navy squadron, managed to negotiate a peace with Tunis. A heavy naval bombardment by the British then brought about a similar peace with Tripoli. However for a few, slavery became more than bearable. Some trades — particularly that of shipwright — were so valuable that an owner might well have rewarded his slave with a gift such as a private villa and mistresses.

Many slaves appear to have endured the horrors of slavery by seeing it as punishment for their sins and as a test of their faith. Masters discouraged conversion because it limited the scope of mistreatment and lowered a slave's resale value. If a slaving party had already snatched so many men it had no more room below deck, it might raid a town and then reappear a few days later to sell captives back to their families. This was usually at a considerable discount from the cost of ransoming someone from North Africa, but it was still far more than peasants could afford.

Farmers usually had no ready money, and no property other than house and land. A merchant was usually willing to take these off their hands at distress prices, but it meant that a captured man or woman came back to a family that was completely impoverished. Most slaves bought their way home only after they had gone through the ordeal of passage to Barbary and sale to a speculator. Wealthy captives could usually arrange a sufficient ransom, but most slaves could not. Illiterate peasants could not write home and even if they did, there was no cash for a ransom.

The majority of slaves therefore depended on the charitable work of the religious orders or charities such as Trinitarians (founded in Italy in 1193) and the Mercedarians (founded in Spain in 1203). These were religious orders established to free Crusaders held by Muslims, but they soon shifted their work to redemption of Barbary slaves, raising money specifically for this purpose. Often they maintained lock boxes outside churches marked "For the Recovery of the Poor Slaves," and clerics urged wealthy Christians to leave money in their wills for redemption. The two orders became skilled negotiators, and usually managed to buy back slaves at better prices than did less experienced liberators. Still, there was never enough money to free many captives. It was common then to bring the freed slaves home and march them through city streets in big celebrations. Such big parades became one of the most characteristic urban spectacles of the period, and had a strong religious orientation. Some of the slaves would turn out and march purposely wearing their old slave rags to emphasize their plight or they dressed in special white costumes to symbolize rebirth. ordeals, especially if they had spent many years in captivity. The ransoming orders had significantly reduced slave populations in Barbary, eventually even inflating slave prices, as more cash chased fewer captives.For centuries, European slaves had lived in fear of the lash themselves, and a great many watched redemption parades of freed slaves, all of whom were white. Slavery was a fate more easily imagined for themselves than for distant Africans.

In the Chronicles of William of Malmesbury. He wrote, "In our mother country, there were once a cruel slave trade in Whites, Directly opposite to the Irish coast, there is a seaport called Bristol, the inhabitants of which frequently sent into Ireland to sell those people whom they had bought up throughout England. They exposed to sell maidens in a state of pregnancy, with whom they they made a sort of mock marriage. There you might see with grief, fastened together by ropes, whole rows of wretched beings of both sexes, of elegant forms, and in the very bloom of youth,-- a sight sufficient to excite pity even in barbarism,-offered for sale to the first purchaser. Accursed deed infamous disgrace, that men acting in a manner which brutal instinct alone would have forbidden should sell into slavey their relatives, nay, even their own off springs". Joseph Morgan put it, 'this I take to be the Time when those Corsairs were in their Zenith'. Morgan noted that he had a List, printed in London in 1682' of 160 British ships captured by Algerians between 1677 and 1680. Considering what the number of sailors who were taken with each ship was likely to have been, these examples translate into a probable 7,000 to 9,000 British men and women taken into slavery during this time.In Columbus, Ohio – A new study by Prof Davis suggests that a million or more European Christians were enslaved by Muslims in North Africa between 1530 and 1780 – a far greater number than had ever been estimated before. Professor Robert Davis an authority on the subject of white slavery developed a unique methodology to calculate the number of white Christians who were enslaved along Africa's Barbary Coast, arriving at much higher slave population estimates than any previous studies had found.

Most other accounts of slavery along the Barbary coast didn't try to estimate the number of slaves, or only looked at the number of slaves in particular cities, Davis said. Most previously estimated slave counts have thus tended to be in the thousands, or at most in the tens of thousands. Where as Davis, by contrast, has calculated that between 1 million and 1.25 million European Christians were captured and forced to work in North Africa from the 1600s to 1700s by slave traders from Algiers, and Tripoli alone (these numbers do not include the European people who were enslaved by Morocco and by other raiders and traders of the Mediterranean Sea coast). "Enslavement was a very real possibility for anyone who travelled in the Mediterranean, or who lived along the shores in places like Italy, France, Spain and Portugal, and even as far north as England and Iceland". "Much of what has been written gives the impression that there were not many slaves and minimizes the impact that slavery had on Europe," Davis said. "Most accounts only look at slavery in one place, or only for a short period of time. But when you take a broader, longer view, the massive scope of this slavery and its powerful impact become clear." It is useful to compare this Mediterranean slavery to the Atlantic slave trade that brought black Africans to the Americas.

Over the course of four centuries, the Atlantic slave trade was much larger – about 10 to 12 million black Africans were brought to the Americas. But from 1500 to 1650, when trans-Atlantic slaving was still in its infancy, more white Christian slaves were probably taken to Barbary than black African slaves to the Americas, according to Davis.

"One of the things that both the public and many scholars have tended to take as given is that slavery was always racial in nature – that only blacks have been slaves. But that is not true," Davis said. "We cannot think of slavery as something that only white people did to black people." Davis concluded that it was religion and ethnicity, as much as race, that determined who became slaves.

For the impact of these attacks were devastating – France, England, and Spain each lost thousands of ships, and long stretches of the Spanish and Italian coasts were almost completely abandoned by their inhabitants. At its peak, the destruction and depopulation of some areas probably exceeded what European slavers would later inflict on the African interior.

Extreme large numbers of sailors were captured and sold into slavery in North Africa. The north African kingdoms wanted slaves to build their palaces. The Barbary pirates also known as the Salee Rovers were a terrible menace to the shipping. They attacked ships and provided the slaves after capturing these sailors into their captivity. It is estimated that they captured over 5000 seamen in one year alone. By the end of the 1600s, the Italian peninsula had by then been prey to the Barbary corsairs for two centuries or more, and its coastal populations had largely withdrawn into walled, hilltop villages or the larger towns like Rimini, abandoning miles of once populous shoreline to vagabonds and freebooters.Many found themselves sold into slavery in the Barbary city of Algiers. The outdoor slave market there was on the Al-Souk al-Kabir (the Great Street of the Souks), a wide thoroughfare lined with markets (souks) throughout which transacted the city. New captives were paraded along the Al-Souk al-Kabir while sellers shouted to attract buyers. Buyers examined their hands to see if they were calloused. (Soft hands indicated a life of ease and wealth, and therefore potential profits in the form of a large ransom.) Buyers also examined male captives' teeth to see if they were fit for work as oarsmen in the galleys (galley slaves were fed only hard tack biscuit).Slaves could find daily life grim. If not assigned the brutal drudgery of the galleys, men bought by the state were employed in hard labour: quarrying stone and hauling it off, working in chain gangs on building sites, turning the grinding wheels in grain mills like draft animals, or cleaning cesspits.

Many slaves were manacled and forced to drag heavy chains behind them and at night, they were locked up in bagnios (slave pens), where they slept on the cold stone floor. If they 'transgressed', they could be punished with the bastinado: slaves were hoisted feet first into the air and the soles of their feet caned mercilessly. Men had to demonstrate their fitness, and were beaten with sticks if they did not comply. Buyers examined their hands to see if they were calloused. (Soft hands indicated a life of ease and wealth, and therefore potential profits in the form of high prices they examined male captives' teeth to see if they were fit for work in the galleys, quarrying stone and working in chain gangs or cleaning cesspits. Many were manacled forced to drag heavy chains behind them, At night, they were locked up in bagnios (slave pens).They slept on the cold stone floor. The best they could hope for was to be purchased by a private buyer and end up in domestic service. Young women slaves were mostly bought for harems. Some were ransomed and a few escaped, but the majority found no way out and ended their lives in miserable captivity. The best they could hope for was to be purchased by a private buyer and end up, essentially, as a domestic servant. Young women were mostly bought for harems and disappeared forever. Men were frequently bought by the state, in which case their lot was most likely hard labour and ill treatment.

A document presented to British parliament, 'The Case of Many Hundreds of Poor English Captives in Algiers together with Some Remedies to Prevent their Increase', describes the prisoners' lot. They "suffer and undergo most miserable slavery" and are "put to daily extreme and difficult labour, but a small supply of bread and water for their food, stripped of their clothes and covering, and their lodging on the cold stones and bricks; but what is more, their extreme hard and savage usage, laden sometimes with great burdens of chains, and shut up in noisome places, commonly adding some hundreds of blows on their bare feet, forcing out the very blood".

At the end of the war in 1713 a large number of Anglo American sailors previously involved in privateering or on naval vessels, found themselves unemployed. They turned en masse to piracy attacking vessels whatever their nationality in the Caribbean, the American eastern sea bound, the west African coast and the Indian Ocean. This launched the climax of the Golden Age of Piracy, during which English island governor complained endlessly about the dangers of the sea routes and of the daily increase of pyrites. Charismatic pirate leaders such as Blackbeard Edward Teach Calico Jack, Racham and Charles Vane became well known names even in England.

The Barbary slaves were housed in large prisons called baños (baths), usually in extremely overcrowded conditions. They were in the main used to row the corsair galleys. Their work was so physically demanding that thousands died or became seriously mentally ill the result of being whilst being chained to the oars in the galleys. During the winter months the galeotti slaves worked on state projects such as the quarrying of stone, building walls or harbour facilities, felling timber and constructing new galleys. Their diet was mainly black bread and water. They were only given one change of clothing every year. Many collapsed from sheer exhaustion or suffered from malnutrition. The White slaves they captured especially from Barbary were usually those from poor families, who had little chance of ever buying back their freedom and most would end their days as slaves in North Africa, dying of starvation, disease, or maltreatment. They were often beaten until they got up and went back to work. Often the female slaves were taken as sexual companions by the pasha and they lived comfortably with him in his harem where they lived out their days in captivity. Though the majority of slaves were bought for their ransom value; while awaiting their release, they worked in the palace as harem attendants. Others worked as agricultural labourers, construction work, or were sellers of goods and water for their master.

Muslim corsairs desecrated and even stole church bells to silence the distinctive voice of Christianity. Although hundreds of thousands of Christian slaves were taken from Mediterranean countries. The effects of Muslim slave raids was felt much further away: it appears, for example, that through most of the 17th century the English lost at least 400 sailors a year to the slavers. Even Americans were not immune. For example, one American slave reported that 130 other American seamen had been enslaved by the Algerians in the Mediterranean and Atlantic just between 1785 and 1793 Roughly 700 Americans were held captive in this region as slaves between 1785 and 1815.

The vast scope of slavery in North Africa has been ignored and minimized, in large part because it is on no one's agenda to discuss what happened. Many of the countries that were victims of slavery, such as France and Spain, would later conquer and colonize the areas of North Africa where their citizens were once held as slaves. Maybe because of this history, Western scholars have thought of the Europeans primarily as "evil colonialists" and not as the victims they sometimes were,

People of the time – both Europeans and the Barbary Coast slave owners – did not keep detailed, trustworthy records of the number of slaves. Well in sharp contrast, there are extensive records that document the number of Africans brought to the Americas as slaves. Historian Prof Davis calculated that about one-fourth of slaves had to be replaced each year to keep the slave population stable, as it apparently was between 1580 and 1680. That meant about 8,500 new slaves had to be captured each year. Overall, this suggests nearly a million slaves would have been taken captive during this period. Using the same methodology, Davis has estimated as many as 475,000 additional slaves were taken in the previous and following centuries. The result is that between 1530 and 1780 there were almost certainly 1 million and quite possibly as many as 1.25 million white, European Christians enslaved by the Muslims of the Barbary Coast.

Davis research into the treatment of these slaves suggests that, for most of them, their lives were every bit as difficult as that of slaves in America. "As far as daily living conditions, the Mediterranean slaves certainly didn't have it better," he said. He points out that there was no check of any kind on cruelty: "There was no countervailing force to protect the slave from his master's violence: no local anti-cruelty laws, no benign public opinion, and rarely any effective pressure from foreign states."

Slaves were not just property, they were infidels, and deserved whatever suffering a master meted out. "all slaves who lived in the bagnos and survived to write of their experiences stressed the endemic cruelty and violence practised there."

The favourite punishment was the bastinado, in which a man was put on his back, and his ankles clamped together and held waist high for a sustained beating on the soles of the feet. A slave might get as many as 150 or 200 blows, which could leave him crippled. Systematic violence turned many men into automatons. Slaves were often so plentiful and so inexpensive, there was no point in caring for them; many owners worked them to death and bought replacements.

At the approach of pirates, passengers often tore off their fine clothes and tried to dress as poorly as possible in the hope their captors would send to their families for more modest ransoms. This effort would be wasted if the pirates tortured the captain for information about passengers. It was also common to strip men naked, both to examine their clothes for sewn-in valuables and to see if any circumcised Jews were masquerading as gentiles.

If the pirates were short on galley slaves, they might put some of their captives to work immediately, but prisoners usually went below hatches for the journey home. They were packed in, barely able to move in the filth, stench, and vermin, and many died before they reached port.

Once in North Africa, it was tradition to parade newly-captured Christians through the streets, so people could jeer at them, and children could pelt them with refuse. At the slave market, men were made to jump about to prove they were not lame, and buyers often wanted them stripped naked again to see if they were healthy. This was also to evaluate the sexual value of both men and women;

white concubines had a high value, and all the slave capitals had a flourishing homosexual underground.

White slavery in the Barbary States was the shame of modern civilisation. The European nations made continual efforts throughout many centuries to procure its abolition and to constantly rescue their subjects from that terrible regime.During the 17th century nearly one million Europeans were enslaved on the Barbary coast.

The most feared of the Barbary pirates were those who had caused so much havoc particularly for the West country merchants and shop owners in the early 1600s were those from Morocco based in Algiers or Tunis who were known as Sale Rovers. These were men who regularly sailed out beyond the Straits with large companies of janis-saries in search of prizes, goods and slaves. These Salees Corsairs attacked ships with their overwhelming firepower prior to boarding the enemy vessels. With their appearance of shaven heads and arms almost naked they terrified their enemies. The weekly slave markets terrified new captives and they were poked, prodded and subjected to ridicule. They were housed in deep dungeons which were filthy, stinking and full of vermin. They all wore heavy iron chains around their ankles they were said to weigh 50 pounds. By the end of his reign in 1625 James 1st had given an amnesty to all pirates which was supported by his son Henry. Some 3000 men had accepted the terms of their pardon from the king.

Many privateers and dissatisfied naval men became known as Barbary pirates. Deserting England joining the Muslim faith and plundering British ships. Most of them had just been privateers, sailing with commissions which authorised them to capture for profit merchant shipping belonging to an enemy. This was an international tradition of state sanctioned piracy which had existed for centuries. These corsair Barbary pirates had included the likes of Robert Walsingham, Sir Henry Mainwaring, Captain John Ward, Henry Morgan and Sir Francis Verney.

Robert Walsingham the fearsome one armed corsair captain from London was captured in Ireland in 1618 and condemned to death then saved his own neck by putting his considerable knowledge of Barbary pirates at king James 1st disposal. By the end of his reign in 1625 King James 1st had given an amnesty to all pirates which was supported by his son Henry. By the end of his reign some 3000 men had accepted the terms of their pardon. The most distinguished of these was Sir Henry Mainwaring. whose route to redemption was accompanied by a seemingly effortless transition from outlaw to senior naval officer. After giving up his life of piracy he went on to become an MP and a master of Trinity House, the guild which looked after the interests of seamen and shipping of England. He became vice admiral of the royal fleet. As a staunch royalist he was to become famous for taking the young prince of Wales to safety in 1645. He joined the kings court at Oxford in 1643. Mainwaring is best remembered for his great storytelling of his pirating exploits.

John Ward commonly called captain Ward was described as very short with little hair and that quite white, bald in front, swarthy face and beard. Speaks little and almost always swears. Drunk from morning to night. Most prodigal and plucky. Sleeps a great deal. Half man, half legend, he was the arch-pirate, the corsair king of popular folk lore. London street balladeers sang of how the most famous pirate in the world terrorised the merchants of France and Spain, Portugal and Venice, and routed the mighty Knights of Malta with his bravery and cunning. Parents scared their children with tales of the demon who feareth neither God nor the Devil. Whose deeds are bad, his thoughts are evil, and scared each other with reports that those who fell into his clutches would be tied back to back and thrown overboard or cut in pieces, or shot to death without mercy. Clergymen in their pulpits thundered that Ward and his renegades would end their days in drunkenness, lechery, and sodomy were really such a bad way to go. This most famous pirate of the world was one among thousands of disenchanted, disempowered sailors who turned to piracy. John, Ward was once called "beyond doubt the greatest scoundrel that ever sailed from England", by the English ambassador to Venice. Ward was a privateer for Queen Elizabeth during her war with Spain; after the end of the war, he became a corsair. With some associates he captured a ship in about 1603 and sailed it to Tunis; then he and his crew converted to Islam. He introduced heavily armed square-rigged ships, used instead of galleys, to the North African area, a major reason for the Barbary's future dominance of the Mediterranean. He died of plague in 1622.

Henry Morgan became a grandiose public figure who was unhappy in his Glamorgan childhood home and as a young man had fled to seek the challenge of the new world of the Caribbean as an indentured servant. Morgan arrived at Barbados in 1655 as a junior officer in Cromwell's forces and took part in the unsuccessful attack on Santo Domingo before taking Jamaica, from the Spanish. In later years Morgan was knighted by King Charles and returned to Jamaica in 1674 as its Lieutenant Governor. Morgan spent the rest of his life in Jamaica in Port Royal. In 1684 he wrote to instruct his London lawyers to sue a publisher who described him as a pirate rather than a privateer consequently he won the sum of £200 in damages. English consuls in Barbary were careful not to refer to corsairs as pirates even though the absence of a treaty rather than the presence of a state of war was enough for those corsairs to justify taking a vessel from a military weak nation. Morgan died on August 25th 1688 aged 53 a very wealthy man indeed, with large sugar plantations and 109 slaves.

Sir Francis Verney was an Englishman of noble blood. His family came from a long and respectable pedigree as Buckinghamshire gentry. He had no previous experience of seamanship. In 1608 he had walked out of his family following a dispute. He went to Morocco and joined a group of mercenaries there who were fighting for Mawlay Zidan, one of the claimants to the Sultanate of Morocco. He was related to the commander of the mercenaries captain John Gifford and also his second in command Phillip Gifford. In 1609 Sir Francis was operating as a pirate and had captured three or four ships from Poole in Dorset. Shortly after London was gossiping that the rumour that Sir Francis Varney had converted to Islam and piracy and that he had also seized wine destined for King James 1st. The king was so alarmed that he despatched a man of war to escort an English merchant convoy en route to the levant and the Venetians reported that the corsairs had recently been joined by a certain Francis Verney, an Englishman of very noble blood who has squandered all his fortune. At the same time Sir Francis Varney was said to be living in Tunis, as part of John Wards entourage. He was soon reduced to living in poverty and deeply in debt to the Turks. The news of his conversion to Islam finally set the seal on a real life on Jacobean morality tale of a wild young man who had made the transition from nobility to outlaw. Sir Francis career as a pirate soon ended He was taken at sea by Sicilians imprisoned as a slave for two years.

Simon Danseker was one of the most prominent renegade pirates operating in the Barbary coast during the early 17th century. He was said to command squadrons in Algiers and Tunis equal to his European counterparts, and represented a formidable naval power. He served as a privateer in the Eighty Years' War and afterwards settled in Marseilles, France, marrying the governor's daughter. In 1607 he stole a ship and sailed for Algiers. Finding himself in the service of Redwan, the Pasha of Algiers, he led a brief but infamous career as a Barbary corsair, where it is sometimes claimed that he introduced the round ship. He *"was made welcome as an enemy of the Spaniards"* and had become one of the taife reisi's leading captains within a year of his arrival. Often bringing Spanish prizes and prisoners to Algiers, he became known as Captain Crazy and Simon The Dancer due to his exploits on the sea. He attacked ships of any nation and made trading in the Mediterranean Sea increasingly difficult for every nation. His fleet quickly grew in power, as he incorporated captured ships into his fleet, and was supplied by Algiers with men and use of their shipyards. He was the first to lead the Algiers out of the Straits of Gibraltar, the farthest distance any had ever successfully navigated. He took at least forty ships and sank many of them during the three years that followed. He became quite rich and lived in an opulent palace. He became acquainted with other pirates such as Englishmen Peter Easton and Jack Ward, and he formed a powerful alliance with Ward. In 1609, while taking a Spanish galleon off Valencia, he used the opportunity to communicate a message to Henri IV and the French court through the Jesuit priests on board. He wished to return to Marseilles, having left his wife and children behind long ago, and wished to be exonerated for his crimes. He was reunited with his family later that year, shortly after arriving in Marseilles with four well-armed warships on November 17, 1609. Welcomed by the Duke of Guise, he presented to him "a present of some Turks, who were at once sent to the galleys" as well as a considerable sum in Spanish gold. In 1615 he was called up by Louis XIII to negotiate the release of French ships being held by Yusuf Dey in Tunis. According to the account of William Lithgow, Dansker was led ashore in a ruse by Yusuf, captured by janissaires, and was beheaded in 1611.

In 1626 Trinity House had reckoned there were 1200 or 1400 English captives at Sale, all or mostly taken in the English Channel. When the ships are full of the kings subjects, the pirates returned to Sal to sell the captives in the common market, and then return for more. Ten years later in 1636 there was a definite air of panic among the merchants and fishing fleets who operated out of the south coast ports of England. Shipowners from Exeter, Dartmouth, Plymouth, Barnstable, Southampton, Poole, Weymouth and Lyme Regis got together and complained to King Charles 1 that over the past few years they had lost an alarming eighty seven vessels to piracy, which along with their cargos were worth £96,700. In addition,1160 English seamen were kept in miserable captivity and the burden of caring for the wives and children of those captives was becoming intolerable. The petitioners begged that the Admiralty would issue letters of marque for taking the pirates, as well as mounting regular patrols of some nimble ships to protect coastal waters. However things did not improve with the loss of a further forty two seamen and two fishing vessels. The merchants again petitioned the King complaining that there were now so many pirates about that seamen were refusing to go to sea and fisher men were refusing to take fish. John Crewkerne told the king to his face that coastal patrols were not sufficient. He was supported at that meeting by Archbishop Land.

Samuel Pepys' diary 8th February 1661 wrote:…."went to the Fleece Tavern to drink; and there we spent till four o'clock, telling stories of Algiers, and the manner of the life of slaves there! And truly Captn. Mootham and Mr. Dawes (who have been both slaves there) did make me fully acquainted with their condition there: as, how they eat nothing but bread and water. … How they are beat upon the soles of their feet and bellies at the liberty of their padron. How they are all, at night, called into their master's Bagnard; and there they lie. How the poorest men do use their slaves best. How some rogues do live well, if they do invent to bring their masters in so much a week by their industry or theft; and then they are put to no other work at all. And theft there is counted no great crime at all".

By the spring of 1717 a vast number of British vessels had been taken by the Barbary Corsairs and their captains and crews were all sent to Meknes to go to sea in chains. These captured ships included The *Constant John*, the *David*, the *Abigal*, the *Catherine* the *Desire*, the *Henry and Mary*, the *George*, the *Sarah*, the *Endevour*, the *Prosperous* the *Union and two fishing boats*.

When British slaves were released from Salee and returned to England in 1721 they were treated to great triumphant celebration when thousands of people gathered on the streets of London.

Buyers who hoped to make a quick profit on a fat ransom examined earlobes for signs of piercing, which was an indication of wealth. It was also common to check a captive's teeth to see if he was likely to survive on a tough slave diet. The European powers were unable to stop the slave traffic though they had a better record of controlling the trade, but there was an increase of white slavery during the Napoleonic wars. But it wasn't until 1815, after two wars against them, that the American sailors were themselves free of the Barbary pirates. Finally after an attack by the British and Dutch in 1816 more than 4,000 Christian slaves were liberated and the power of the Barbary pirates was broken.

In 1716 Thomas Pellow a young Cornish cabin boy was amongst a group of sailors captured at sea by Captain Ali Hakem and his band of slave traders of the Barbary Corsairs. Young Thomas and his comrades had now become the property of the sultan of Morocco Moulay Ismail. Moulay Ismail took a liking to the young Thomas and he was chosen by him for special attention. Thomas Pellow was to became the sultans personal slave for some 23 years. During those years he was to witness first hand the barbarism, terrors alongside the splendid surroundings of the sultans imperial court and palace. Out of all the many thousands of white European Christians who suffered under the slavery of that regime. He was one of the few slaves amongst the 3,000 who were captives when he arrived. He survived and later lived to tell his own story.

In the summer of 1738, after escaping he returned to England aged thirty-three .

After initially arriving in London, he journeyed on to Cornwall and in October was finally reunited with his parents and greeted with a hero's welcome. His unbelievable story had been picked up by the newspapers and many in the local community were in awe of his return as stories such as his did not usually have a happy ending. Thomas Pellow could finally, after twenty-three years breathe a sigh of relief; his ordeal was over, his freedom secure and the threat to his life no more. A couple of years later he would pen his memoirs in a best-selling novel entitled, "The History of the Long Captivity and Adventures of Thomas Pellow" which provided an enthralling and compelling account of slavery, Islamic culture and the kingdom of Morocco.

White Gold by Giles Milton.
Hodder and Stoughton.

CHAPTER SIX

GALLEY SLAVES

The Awakening

Awake for all those mourning in the bowels of life
have stranded freedom
In the slavery of flight
adorn your hearty and kindred prayers
in words of fancy suppressed and wanton cares
break up those thoughts which lay hidden
in the darkest caverns of ones mind
no longer can one shudder at the perils of the deep
within the galleys where the oars lie thick with sweat
down to ones so sad feet
oh freedom offers sanctuary from such bliss
like the lovers first sensual moist erotic kiss
share no more your sad and sodden grasp of infinity
celebrate the freedom of that lovers kiss with me

Ray Wills

Slave trades

Down in the galleys
feet in the stocks
the ships in the harbour
all slaves on the docks

Seagulls above us
up in the sky
worries and crimes
futures afore us
turn of the tides
pass us all bye

The weight of the oars
and the captain on deck
we sail to the plantations
sugar and red legs
sweat in our brows
runs down our necks

Ships calls its leaving
tides out and more
sail to new shores
suns in the sky
eyes on the floor

With wet feet and aches
sweat on our brows
living the promise

till the morrow

There are clouds in the sky
for the crimes that we did
for being in need
our hungers and sorrows
our mouths for to feed

It was down in the meadows
out in the trees
we were caught poaching rabbits and pheasants
hear the game keepers pleas

The masters and gentry
amidst those halls of the kings
lords of the oceans
youl hear our loud screams

The whips on our backs
in our shackles and chains
just a man and a number
no name just shame

To work on the lords lands
plantations so big
cutting the beet
with the irons and chains
cutting into my feet

Working from daybreak
onto the dark
no sleep for the wicked
prayers for the master
just food for the sharks

Ray Wills

Pathways to Heaven

On the pathways to heaven
in those grand gardens of shame
where the rich and the poor men
all said that their all not to blame

For the cruelty and horrors
and the weapons of war
where the good Lord counts blessings
in the grace of his word

All the human cattle
and their shepherds of shame
amidst the flocks of their game
all the castaway indentured servants
and the men with no names

The books they were opened
and the names they were read
for the sorrows of angels
to all the new born
the living and dead

Gabriel blew a trumpet
and made the sign of the cross
all the fine words were granted to fools
and the victories lost such a cost

To the wings of the angels
and the flight of the free

amidst all the ships on the waves
in the lands over the seas

The captain called for freedom
and the children they all laughed
whilst the virgins were all a sleeping
and the clowns took a bath

The crowds they were so many
when they counted up the score
when the slave ships all set sail
far off from those foreign shore

The wedding was over then
and the bride kissed the groom
there was thunder and lightning that night
beneath the bright Barbados moon

The crafts they set sail
and the captains were blessed
by the sermon of prophets
yet they held all their shameful secrets
close to their chests

For the flock it was safe now
the victors were all set free
from the chains of the slavery trade
in a world of mere promises
from the perils at sea

Ray Wills

A great many Gypsies were taken as galley slaves throughout the centuries. A galley was a type of ship that is propelled mainly by rowing. They were used by various civilisations around the Mediterranean from the Phoneticans to the Romans and Greek. The Vikings raided across Europe, but took the most slaves in raids on the British Isles and in Eastern Europe. They kept some slaves as servants, but they sold most captives in the Byzantine or Islamic markets. In the West, their target populations were primarily English, Irish, and Scottish. These Viking slave-traders had settled in the 11th century in the European territories they had once raided and they themselves eventually merged with the local populace. There was an excessive demand for European slaves in the wealthy Muslim empire of Northern Africa and Spain, Soon there was a market for these slaves which became so lucrative that it created a great economic boom in central and western Europe, today known as the Carolingian Renaissance. This boom in demand for slaves lasted throughout the early Muslim conquests. It ended as the Islamic Golden Age waned. The Order of the Knights of Malta attacked pirates and Muslim shipping, and their base became a centre for slave trading, selling captured North African and Turks. Malta was to remain a slave market until well into the late 18th century. One thousand slaves were required to man the galleys (ships) of the Order of the knights of Malta. Medieval Spain and Portugal saw almost constant warfare between Muslims and Christians. They sent periodic raiding expeditions to loot the Iberian Christian kingdoms, bringing back booty and slaves. In a raid against Lisbon, Portugal in 1189, 3,000 females and children were taken captive. In a subsequent attack upon Silves, Portugal in 1191, the governor of Cordoba took 3,000 Christian slaves. North African pirates abducted and enslaved more than 1 million Europeans between 1530 and 1780 in a series of raids that depopulated coastal towns from Sicily to Cornwall in England. As a result thousands of white Christians were seized every year to work as galley slaves, labourers and concubines for Muslim overlords in what is today Morocco, Tunisia, Algeria and Libya, it is claimed. A galley slave was a slave rowing in a galley, either a criminal who was being punished or a prisoner of war. Even common criminals such as petty thieves were sent to the galleys, along with smugglers and murderers. Marginalized social groups such as Gypsies or paupers were also taken as galley slaves along with army deserters if they were captured. They were all branded with the letters GAL to identify them and they were called the Gallérians. From 1580 to 1680 there were around 8,500 new slaves a year, totalling 850,000 and 475,000 were abducted in the previous and following centuries. According to one estimate, 7,000 English people were abducted between 1622-1644, many of them ships' crews and passengers. But the corsairs also landed on unguarded beaches, often at night, to snatch the unwary. By the 1600s King Louis XIV of France had decided to increase the number of his vessels to 40 making it the largest galley fleet in the Mediterranean. The king got many thousands of rowers to man his 40 vessels. Colbert informed magistrates of the king's wish that they "condemn the greatest number of criminals possible and that even the death penalty be converted to that of the galleys." The King banned Protestantism from France in 1685 and over 1500 followers, called Huguenots, were condemned to the galleys for refusal to convert to Catholicism or tried to flee the country. Louis XIV's galleys were beautiful and extravagant but the galley slaves paid the price. 450 rowers were packed onto the ship's deck, which was less than 150 feet long and 30 feet wide. Space was so cramped that the men could not even bend their arms while pulling the oars. They lived in terrible conditions so even if they had a short sentence, most rowers would eventually die from the lack of food and sleep. Galleys are very low in the water and were not suited to high seas and strong waves. A good-sized merchantman might yield 20 or so sailors healthy enough to last a few years in the galleys. Earlier in 1660 Polish pilgrims visiting a sanctuary in France were forcibly enlisted! Others included were deserters from the army who, after capture, were given a life sentence on the galleys. Runaways had their nose and ears mutilated, their cheeks branded with the fleur-de-lis, and their head shaved. Most of these public slaves spent the rest of their lives as galley slaves. Men were chained three, four, or five to an oar, with their ankles chained together as well. Rowers never left their oars, and to the extent that they slept at all, they slept at their benches. Slaves could push past each other to relieve themselves at an opening in the hull, but they were often too exhausted or dispirited to move, and fouled themselves where they sat. They had no protection against the burning Mediterranean sun, and their masters flayed their already-raw backs with the slave driver's favourite tool of encouragement, a stretched bull's penis or "bull's pizzle." There was practically no hope of escape or rescue; a galley slave's job was to work himself to death — mainly in raids to capture more wretches like himself — and his master pitched him overboard at the first sign of serious illness. Every slave had his place and worked to his maximum capacity. So slaves were chained in their place to not leave that area and were controlled by an overseer with a whip. time was at its peak.In the Christian slave ships, paupers so destitute that they had sold themselves to the galleys captains. It was these wretches, chained three or four to a foot wide bench, who made sea wars possible. Their sole function was to work themselves to death. Shackled hand and foot, excreting where they sat, fed on meagre quantities of black biscuits and so thirsty that they were themselves resolved to drink sea water, the galley slaves could expect a short and bitter life. The men naked apart from a pair of linen breeches, were flayed raw by the sun, sleep deprivation on the narrow bench propelled them to towards madness, the strole keepers drum and the overseers lash. a tarred rope or a dried bulls penis-whipped them beyond the point of exhaustion during the long stretches of intensive efforts when a ship was trying to capture or escape from another vessel. The Englishman Joseph Morgan wrote, "That least tolerable and most to be dreaded ranks and files of half naked, half starved, half tanned, meagre wretches, chained to a plank from whence they remove once for months at a time-urged on even beyond human strength, with cruel and repeated blows, on the bare flesh".

Up to 450 rowers could be packed on a ship's deck—less than 150 feet long and 30 feet wide. They lived and worked in this cramped environment for months at a time. Some spent their life, twenty years as galley slaves. Their skin became ulcerated from the salty sea air, and their bodies bore the scars of frequent beatings. Half would die in what French historians call France's "greatest spoiler of men." In the Middle Ages, galley rowers—or *galeotti,* as they were called—were freemen, and rowing was considered an honorable profession. However by the 17th century, things had changed considerably. Turks, were purchased as rowers from the Ottoman Empire. Most were Muslims, although some were adherents of Orthodoxy. There were also many Prisoners of war amingst them. They "condemned the greatest number of criminals possible and so that even the death penalty was to be converted to that of the galleys." The number sent to the galleys during the reigns of Louis XIV and his great-grandson Louis XV was without precedent. Between 1680 and 1748, about 60,000 men were condemned to row there. Up to half of them were common criminals, vagrants, murderers to petty thieves. Smugglers were also among them . These socially marginalized individuals were forced to man the galleys. In 1666 the officer in charge of them in Marseilles wrote: "I would like a decision to be made to take the lazy, the pilgrims, the Gypsies, and other wanderers and fill up whole galleys with them.... That would clean the world of its burdensome filth." Thus, under the pretext of maintaining public order, Gypsies and paupers were recruited as galley slaves. (Extract - Watchtower online).The volumes hold a magnifying glass up to 17th- and 18th-century society, which treated crimes related to money or certain sexual practices more harshly than murder. Francisco Giménez, "Gypsy, native of the land of Segura, son of Sebastián Moreno, both ears cut," was sentenced to eight years on the galleys for a crime. But Juan de Morales, 35 years old, "native of Utrera, son of Pedro, good constitution, white, blue eyes," was given 200 lashes and 10 years on the galleys for committing "the unspeakable sin" - which is to say, sodomy.

During the numerous wars of that era 1685 to 1715, about 17,000 deserters were sent to the galleys. The galley rowers' suffering began even before going to sea. Initially, they were left in temporary prisons for up to six months before being chained with hundreds of others and dragged to Marseilles. For some, such as those sent from Brittany or Paris, a forced march over 500-mile journey nightmare lasting over a month. Many died on the road. During the journey they endured beatings and were deprived of food and sleep whilst people along the route showed little sympathy for them. Many of those had never seen the sea, let alone galleys. Arrival at the port of Marseilles, was a rude awakening. They were herded onto an empty galley and examined, as one of them wrote, like "cows purchased at the market." Personal details were recorded, and the prisoners became numbers in the galley system. "Entry into the society of galley rowers no doubt caused extreme disorientation and was a huge psychological and physical shock," notes a historian. The French Crown had filled its galleys with French Huguenots, Protestants condemned for resisting the state. Galley slaves lived and worked in such harsh conditions that many did not survive their terms of sentence, even if they survived the shipwrecks and slaughters or torture at the hands of enemies or of pirates.

Galley slaves were packed on a ship's deck—less than 150 feet long and 30 feet wide—were 450 rowers. They lived and worked in this cramped environment for months at a time. Their skin became ulcerated from the salty sea air, and their bodies bore the scars of frequent beatings. Half would die in what French historians call France's "greatest spoiler of men."

The gallery compartments measured just seven and a half feet by four feet. For months at a time five men lived here and rowed, all chained to their benches. Each rower had a space of just a foot and a half in which to sit. Space was so cramped that the men could not even bend their arms while pulling the oars, each of which measured at least 39 feet in length and each weighed over 280 pounds. Rowing for hours at a time was backbreaking work that tore the rowers' muscles, greatly taxing their strength and stamina. It was "comparable to the most difficult tasks performed in a tropical climate," explains a historian. Galleys were low-lying, and the rowers were only about three feet above the waterline. As a result they often rowed with their feet in water, with their skin eaten by the salty air. Food rations were meagre. "Convicts would do anything to survive," notes a historian. Escape was almost out of the question. The bounty placed on the head of escapees motivated local peasants to join the hunt for any who tried to get away. Only 1 in 100 were ever successful.

The sentences were rarely respected. Thus, a rower condemned for a few years might find himself still at the oar some 25 years later. About a third of the men died within three years. Overall, half the rowers did not survive. Mortality was just as high for the rowers on land as at sea. During the winter of 1709/10, one third of galley slaves died due to famine and the extreme weather. Tragically, some had been sent to the galleys just because of their religion.Eventually, the galleys drifted into oblivion, victims of naval realities and a lack of funding. King Louis financial problems resulted in cutbacks. By 1720, only 15 of his boats remained, and their activity was greatly reduced. Much of the time, galley rowers stayed in Marseilles, where they became part of the city's economic scene, working in nearby soap factories or selling the clothes that they knitted.

Between 1680 and 1748, about 60,000 men were condemned to row. Up to half of those sent to the galleys were common criminals. They ranged from murderers to petty thieves. Smugglers were also punished in this way, at times making up a large number of those who manned the oars. In addition, socially marginalized individuals were forced to man the galleys. Finally, in 1748 a law was passed that in effect sounded the galleys' death knell. Indeed, the memory of the galley slaves remains a powerful testimony to the terrible injustices that humans have inflicted on their fellow men.

CHAPTER SEVEN

THE PRESS GANGS

It was said that those now pressed into the navy consisted mostly of "'vagrants, Gipsies, those living at the charge of the parish [recipients of Poor Law relief], the maimed, the halt and sundry idiots." In short, "the sweepings of the borough."

Cavalier Island

There is a cavalier island with boats in each bay
with men on the side walks youl meet them each day
the streets and the alleys the pubs and the inns
the oaths tat they swear there with whiskey and gin

There were faraway people with love in their eyes
with thoughts of the future and free enterprise
the lights from the beacons the masts on the hill
the meadows of comfort and the sounds of their tills

The boys and the gals there with long flowing hair
their wisdom is special with beauty and care
there's sailors and vessels and winds that blow free
with annuals of dreams lost out at sea

The shadows you meet there are distant old friends
with words you can trust around the next bend
there's sorrows and fortitude with springs flowing free
with song of the song thrush and buzz of the bees

So don't pack your bags now or ride of this trail
where moonlight evades one and memories dwell
there's fun and there's laughter a plenty this day
just follow your dreams and il be on my way

Ray Wills

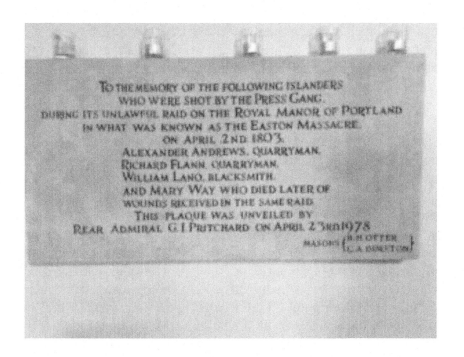

Press gangs or impressment was originally a practice used way back in the 13th Century, in the Elizabethan age. It was then a means of clearing the streets of ever-rising numbers of vagrants the unemployed and undesirables. Its practice was now enforced once again following the Napoleonic war in 1815. As many as three quarters of the British Navy were to consist of such impressed men or press gangs. The developments in naval gunnery meant that merchant ships were no longer suitable for use in fighting. Instead governments maintained a fleet of specialist warships that would be manned with sailors drawn from merchant ships when war broke out.

The legal basis for Impressment (the formal name for the practice of the press gangs.) was that during times of war, the crown had the right to call on the services of merchant vessels and their crews and these powers were formally laid down in an Act of Parliament "touching political considerations for the maintenance of the navy" in 1563.Throughout 1700s and early 1800s there were seven major wars. Culminating in Great Britain's involvement against Napoleon' at the Battle of Trafalgar in 1805. The British Navy needed to increase their numbers drastically with able bodied men ready to man their warships. The Navys solution was to revert to an old action known as impressment or to create press gangs. The Act of 1740 stated that those liable to be pressed should be seafarers, between the ages of 18 and 55, and either British citizens, foreigners married to British women, or foreign nationals who had served for a minimum of two years on a British ship. Landsmen, apprentices and "gentlemen" were excluded, as were those carrying certificates of exemption – such as dockyard workers. The act also supplied the authorities with a convenient loophole, however. In time of crisis, it gave the Admiralty the right to order a "hot press," when these restrictions could be ignored, without fully defining what constituted a "crisis."The means of recruitment of these impressed men during these years was often traumatic and chaotic experience as many men were stolen away from their families and community. Often without warning or any time in which to settle their home affairs at home. Men in seafaring trades faced the terrifying prospect that at almost any moment a press gang could turn up at their home or harbour local inn and seize them, The press gang could beat them if they resisted, and then drag them away to a life in the navy that they may only return from if they were lucky.The popular image of press-gangs is of an underhand recruiting sergeant in a dockside tavern plying patrons with drink then surreptitiously slipping a 'King's Shilling' into their tankard as payment for their 'volunteering' into the Navy, before carrying off the hapless, possibly legless fellow to a life of squalid brutality onboard a RN warship. Tankards were made with glass bottoms because of this subterfuge so that the drinker could see if a coin was in there before he 'accepted payment' in drinking its contents. This is a misconception, however.Although the Navy did prefer volunteers (by any means) rather than pressed men during the more placid interludes of empire building the rate the Navy dwindling manpower meant press gangs could take almost any man they thought suitable, and their victim was more likely to get a whack over the head with a club than a shilling.

Though laws were eventually enacted to limit impressment to seafaring professions, and in theory apprentices and foreigners were exempt. In times of national emergency or if the press gang was unscrupulous (they received bounties for every pressed man) these parameters were often overlooked. Impressment at the time was 100% legal.

There was little a man could do to avoid impressment, save run or fight. Life in the navy was a horrid and brutal one and compared badly to the pay and conditions in Britain's merchant fleets.

Unlike Napoleon's massive Grande Armee which employed widespread conscription, provoking discord nationwide as a result, British people were spared conscription, and were left largely free to enjoy their God-given liberties because a large navy requires a lot less manpower than a large army.

Impressment; a system of forced military service was much more selective than conscription, but for those eligible for military service recruitment was a much more traumatic and chaotic experience; men were stolen away without warning or time to settle affairs at home beforehand.Men in seafaring trades faced the terrifying prospect that at almost any moment a press gang could turn up and seize them, beat them if they resisted, and then drag them away to a life in the navy that they may only return from if they were lucky. All family and friends could do was cry and curse in their wake as a father, husband or son was taken away, for the press gang cared little for the suffering their actions heaped on households who were about to lose the main bread-earner, leaving them destitute in the process. Most of the impressed men were actually taken from merchant ships just before they returned from long voyage, looking forward to seeing their families again only to be taken away to spend several more years away from home. The trauma this must have imposed on the men and their families can only be imagined. Fathers, husbands and sons were taken away, for the press gang cared little for the suffering of their actions. As a result many households lost their main bread-earner., \It was a process which left many of their families destitute in the process. Though most impressed men were actually taken from merchant ships just before they returned from long voyage, looking forward to seeing their families again only to be taken away to spend several more years at sea.The need for labour in the Virginia plantations and West Indies also at the time encouraged planters and their agents to "press gang" unwary or naïve locals onto ships, bound for the Americas. Then once at their destination, these people were indentured to plantation owners against their will. They were released eventually, unlike Africans similarly employed. Many made enough money to buy passage back to Scotland, whence they had come. These actions were justified on the basis that the persons in question were labelled as indigent, and under a 1652 law such people could be deported to overseas colonies. Impressment by the press gangs was the scourge of maritime communities throughout Britain and all its North American colonies. The official bands of thugs of press gangs were headed by naval officers who were sent ashore from Royal Navy (RN) warships. Their instructions were to enter inns where they were to entice and kidnap the King's subjects to serve on the high seas. Although the Navy did prefer volunteers rather than pressed men. The press gangs often took any man they thought suitable. Their victim was more likely to suffer from a whack over the head from a club than te offer of a shilling in their drink. Press gangs were totally legal at the time. Unscrupulous members of such press gangs could gain cash bounties for every pressed man. There was unfortunately little an unwilling volunteer could do to avoid impressment apart from fighting back or fleeing.Reports of sailors and townsfolk banding together were rampant to fight off these despised gangs of marauding thugs, and often many were quite successful. Most however presumably accepted their fates, but not everyone. Some tried to flee in desperation: As the following tales dictate."Friday morning a press gang having information that several sailors were secreted in a house in Orchard Street, Westminster, entered it, and one man, in endeavouring to escape from the top of the house, fell into the yard upon the top of a pump, and was killed on the spot."

A story of one man's desperate escape in a fishing village in 18th Century Ireland: "A press gang crashed into the 'Mc Alpin's Suir Inn' and a young fellow ran out the door, fled into a neighbour's house, jumped through a window and landed in the lap of the house owner's daughter. She started to scream and he gagged her and the house owner came in and said 'it's either the press gang or my daughter'. So, he chose the daughter. But for years afterwards when he'd get drunk in McAlpin's at the bar, he'd mumble into his pint 'I should've went with the press gang.'"As the ideas of liberty in the Age of Enlightenment took hold, there was an ever fiercer conflict between one's concept of duty and individual sovereignty, illustrated by an anecdote by the famous French philosopher Voltaire who told of the time he found a Thames waterman, who had been boasting about the liberty of Englishmen, confined the next day in a prison cell by the press gang. While the idea of a Press Gang may seem barbaric to us today, the concept of forced participation in warfare was common practice at the time. Captain James Nicholson, who commanded USS Virginia was forced to release thirty sailors from Baltimore that he had seized in 1777. He subsequently completed his crew by taking sailors from American merchant ships he encountered at sea.The Times' newspaper from 1790 reported the following account -"Friday night, about 10 o'clock, a press gang made their appearance in Oxford market — As they were carrying off a butcher's lad, they were beset by a large party of the sons of the cleaver, and received so complete a drubbing [beating], that they were glad to relinquish their prisoner, and shelter themselves in a beer-house in Berwick-Street, the Lieutenant narrowly escaping with his life." "Monday, as four sailors, who had returned from sea a few days before, were drinking in a public-house in Atherton Street, Liverpool, they were attacked by a press gang, but the sailors having fire-arms with them, warned the gang to keep off; This they did not attend to, and were coming to seize the sailors, when they fired, and one of the press gang was killed upon the spot, and another very dangerously wounded."As the need for manpower on ships grew, some of the excesses of press gangs began to appear. Fights could break out, particularly when the press gangs instituted a "hot press" and ignored the usual protections against the impressment of non-seamen. In 1803 a press gang raided the village of Easton on the Isle of Portland in Dorset, attempting to take quarrymen. They were opposed by an angry crowd which they fired on, killing four people.

One tale from Wales in 1803 tells of Six defendants appeared in court one day charged with assaulting the officer of a press gang who was carrying out his duty. Two were identified as mariners, another two were farm labourers who'd never been to sea but one had been friends with one of the mariners. There was an additional mariner who'd just returned home from a two-year voyage to the Caribbean. The last defendant had been dragged from his home leaving a wife and two small children. All six were convicted and handed over to the press gang to join the fleet. Another defendant was charged and convicted of stealing a brass pan from a field. He was also sentenced to be sent to sea. Though some of the impressed sailors were scoundrels or wasters many more were decent respectable working men, as this press report recorded:In 1808, Thomas Urquhart, a gentleman, was saved by passers-by from the press gang who tried to seize him in a London street. Urquhart went on to campaign against the evils of manning the navy in this way.There was no limit to the audacity of these press gangs: A letter from Margate says 'Last night a naval officer landed on the pier about ten o'clock with a press gang, and having exercised his authority in a manner deemed improper by the high constable and another peace officer of this port, they interfered and informed the naval officer that the persons he had impressed were not objects of the impress act. In consequence of this interference, the gang seized the two constables, and sent them with several others on board the ship.'"The French philosopher Voltaire told of the time he found a Thames waterman, who had been boasting about the liberty of Englishmen, confined the next day in a prison cell by the press gang. Reports were common of sailors and townsfolk banding together to fight off these despised gangs of marauding press gang thugs, and often quite successfully.'The press gang is deeply imbedded in our perception of the 18th century Royal Navy. The popular view is of warships, ever hungry for manpower, sending club-wielding thugs to raid sleepy coastal villages at dawn, or to round up the inebriated from taverns to be taken away to a life at sea. Yet many songs of the time, like Rule Britannia composed in 1740 and Hearts of Oak in 1759 make much of the navy as a defender of British freedom. How ironic that freedom should come at the expense of the liberty of her citizens? Numerous acts were implemented; each formally refined the limits of who could be taken.

Most European powers had conscription for both army and navy, so that in some ways Britain restricting the use of compulsion to just sailors might be regarded as quite mild. Indeed conscription – the modern equivalent of impressment – was used by all sides in both World Wars, and remains in place in some countries, such as Switzerland, Austria and Finland, to this day. The numbers of impressed sailors could be large, and the proportion grew steadily as the Royal Navy expanded. In the Seven Years War the evidence is that impressment was mainly used to top up numbers, with about a quarter of sailors being pressed. By the Napoleonic Wars this figure had risen to be over half. Naval historians also suspect that many of those listed as 'volunteering' may have done so to avoid the threat of impressment. Men who volunteered gained several useful advantages, including exemption from debt, a signing on bonus, and some say over which ship they would serve on.Impressment also caused friction with Britain's North American colonies. It was listed as one of the colonial grievances in the run up to the War of Independence, and was a major issue in the War of 1812. Ironically the US Continental Navy went on to have many of the same manning issues, when they found themselves unable to compete with the wages on offer to sailors who joined US privateers, and had to resort to some impressment of their own. Fortunately as Britan's mastery over the world after 1830, along with a large increase in population and with better working conditions in the RN this put an end to the scourge of the press gangs impressment for good.The end of the Napoleonic War saw the abandonment of the use of impressment. Britain would not fight another major naval war for decades, by which time the navy was able to man itself with volunteers. This was driven mainly by the degree of specialism and training that was now required onboard modern warships. An 18th century sailing warship was essentially a scaled-up version of a sailing merchantman, but the same could not be said of a steam-powered ironclad. This forced the navy to resort to more imaginative solutions to the manning problem, such as properly trained long service volunteers and the formation of a naval reserve.

CHAPTER EIGHT

THE JEWEL IN THE CROWN

"The conditions were that the convicts should be carried beyond the sea as slaves, that they should not be emancipated for ten years, and that the place of their banishment should be some West Indies Island. This last article was studiously framed for the purpose for the purpose of aggravating their misery".

Lord Macauley, History of England

SLAVES AND MASTERS

The heat of the sun and the scorching G on my brow
the cutting of my flesh from the irons and chains
the call of the black masters echoes refrains
the ships standing by with their sails and the dames

The plantations awaiting us on the journeys with its galleys and
rum
the price of the slaves yet their freedom to come
the sounds of the bargaining barters and the masters with pens
with their waistcoats and breeches so fancy
the sun of the decks

The sweat on our brows with the pain of the shackles and holds
the cries of the young men and the wails of the old
the watches and purses of the masters all to declare
their bargains to board the ships amidst the cries of despair
all the handshakes of gentlemen with their coins set in dust
poor cosseted Gypsies with no one to trust

The hurt and the tears and the screech of the gulls
the histories of mankind without any love
the trades and the bartering on the tragedy blocks
all for their Lords with their rubies and common bucks
bound for far distant journeys with only the sounds of the Gypsies

Kushti Bok

Ray Wills

Barbados in the West Indies has a chequered history. It was first discovered by the Portugal Pedro a Campos. Before being taken by the Spanish in 1492. Barbados was originally owned by a single person, Sir William Courteen, a merchant from London. It was he who made a claim to the island and acquired the title to it from the crown. Therefore, the first colonists to live on Barbados were actually Courteen's tenants, and a large portion of the profits of their labour there were given to him and his company. A decree issued in 1625 had mandated that Irish political prisoners be transported overseas and sold to English settlers in the West Indies. The captain of the British ship *The Olive Blossom*, John Powell had claimed the island for king James 1st. The Spaniards had previously enslaved and wiped out the native Carib Indians leaving Barbados for the larger Caribbean islands. The British merchants were one of the main participants in the Atlantic slave trade. The Island of Barbados was initially known as the Tobacco Island. Barbados not only became the most populated of England's overseas colonies, but also one of the most heavily populated colonies in the world. Barbados also played a leading role in the all of the settlement of the West Indies.

William Courteen maintained ownership of the island until 1629 when his title was transferred by the new King to James Hay, the 1st Earl of Carlisle. James Carlisle chose Henry Hawley as governor of the island, a move made to appease the residents there who might otherwise have opposed his ownership of the island, as it was widely believed among English settlers on Barbados that Carlisle stole the title from Courteen.In February 1627, a party of eighty English settlers and ten slaves had settled on Barbados where they founded a colony at Holetown (formerly known as Jamestown). Thereby erasing away any traces of the original inhabitants, known as the Arawaks, who had lived there for centuries.

When Captain John Powell landed at Barbados his party erected a cross at the site which was later to become St James Town with an inscription nearby on a tree which read "James King of England and this island".

Only people with good financial backgrounds and social connections with England were accepted as a planter. Barbados had many common nick names from "The Jewel in the Crown", to "Litttle England" and "the white graveyard". Land was allocated to speculators and within a few years, much of the island had been deforested to make way for tobacco and cotton plantations.

Much of the early capital to finance White slavery in the British West Indies came from Sephardic Jews from Holland who provided credit, machinery and shipping facilities. The rich yung men were allocated land in this new colony; in the main these were regarded as gentlemen class with Barbados's strong connection and staunchly British attitude which had earned it the original title of Little England.

The production of tobacco and cotton was heavily reliant on poor, uneducated labourers who were enlisted from England, Scotland and throughout Europe. Despite the fact that it was stated by the laws of Barbados that these labourers could not be enslaved, they were still seen as being the property of their slave masters.

However, following the poor gains from tobacco and cotton. Sugar cane was introduced on the island and was soon to become the islands major industry.

The English turned Barbados into a slave society, a slave economy, which would be replicated in several parts of the "new world". It was the birthplace of British slave society and the most ruthlessly colonised by the ruling elite who made their fortunes from sugar produced by an enslaved people. A great wealth created in the sugar plantations secured Britain's place as an imperial superpower and at the same time and by doing so it caused untold suffering.

A system of indenture, was developed by the Virginia company in the 1620s whereby young men and women contracted themselves to work for a master for a period ranging from three to nine years. In return they were given passage to the colonies and subsistence during their tenure. Some were paid annual wages, but most were promised a one off payment – usually around 10 pounds or some land such as in Barbados it was 10 acres. At the end of their contact. Barbadian planters had at first used white British labourers as indentured servants to work on their farms.

The term Indentured servants meant that labourers would work for their employers for free for a fixed length of time in return for being granted their freedom and given some land at the end of their service. Many Irish people travelled to America and the Caribbean under these terms. Many of them were treated badly and even betrayed at the end of their service when the landowner reneged on the deal. However, Jordan and Walsh claim that the cruelty and injustice went further than this. They say many of these indentured servants were effectively slaves. They also believe that thousands more Irish people were transported to the Caribbean from the 1600s up to the 1800s, not to work as indentured servants, but to be sold into a lifetime of slavery.A reference dated November, 1665, comments upon the motives for indenturing Gypsies and others in this way: The light regard paid to the personal right of individuals was shown by a wholesale deportation of poor people at this time to the West Indies out of a desire as to promote the Scottish and English plantations in Jamaica and Barbados for the honour of their country, as to free the kingdom of the burden of many strong and idle beggars, Egyptians, common and notorious thieves, and other dissolute and loss persons banished and stigmatised for gross crimes (Chambers, 1858:304).Some 30,000 indentured servants went to the Caribbean during these early years with a similar figure going to the North American colonies. Amongst them were dissenters and politically disaffected, but most consisted of members of the rural poor suffering from the severe economic and social troubles in England at that time. Most were from the West country, Anglia and Ireland, often tricked by merchants or middleman into selling their labour, or even kidnapped. Others sold themselves out of sheer desperation. But a large number saw it as an opportunity, particularly the young and those with energy and who saw emigration as a means to improve themselves for good as a route to freedom of religion politics or economise. Few however knew just what they had actually let themselves in for.

Indentured workers actually worked for far longer they could and were often sold on by their masters and were unable to negotiate their own contract and rarely bettered themselves. These indentured "servants" were to be given, by decree of the King, ten pounds in either money or goods upon being granted their freedom, and before the mid-1630's, they were to also receive a few acres of land – But none of this was never upheld and there are no records of any indentured servant in this period receiving this entitlement. This was due to the fact that the existing Planters (or gentry) had already laid claim to all available land.

The three main types of indentured workers were:

1) Freewiller, those who sold themselves, under indenture,

2) Redemptioner were those who were persuaded or duped into signing up and who were sold for cash on arrival and

3) Spiriters who were those who were taken/ kidnapped by merchants or ships captains or press ganged which operated in theBritish ports such as Bristol, Liverpool, London, Weymouth, Poole etc. Many of these kidnapped included very young children. One of the kidnappers boasted he had sold an average of 500 children a year over a period of twelve years. Another that he had captured and sold 850 in a single year. The agents and merchants used every means to instigate working class people to transport to Barbados.

By 1645 more than 11,000 white farmers of English stock were established on the island, owning around 6,000 slaves, and most of these were growing third rate tobacco. These early planters bought their slaves from the Dutch slave trades. Initially the slaves were permitted to build their own poor homes but as sugar became plentiful this soon ended. Within just 2 years there were 74 sugar plantation owners who had 80,000 slaves. Barbados was now twenty times richer than it had ever been prior to the coming of sugar. The price of land was even more remarkable, for 500 acres in 1640 sold for £400 now fetched £7,000 for just half that size. Barbados soon became the natural lodge gate to the Americas. It was used by the North American colonialists ,who were soon to buy all manner of goods there including slaves. The white tobacco farmers who did not change over to sugar production lost almost everything. Most of them emigrated mainly to America whilst others survived becoming the future red legs. The planters who carried out this sugar revolution such as the young James Drax, eventually returned to homes in England as very rich gentlemen. Their families began to think of their Caribbean sugar empires as if they were gold mines.

Life on Barbados was hard at this time in history. Parish records from the mid-1600's on Barbados show four times as many deaths as marriages on the island. Residents were continually being replaced by new arrivals. Colonial officials passed a law in 1636 that formalized the status of the African and Amerindian slaves including their offspring, as the property of white settlers. This law stated that all slaves brought to Barbados, both Afrikan and Amerindian must be enslaved for life. As a consequence, Barbados became a nation of masters and slaves with a minority of Jews, poor whites and freed coloureds.

In Barbados throughout the 1600s European indentured servants were the main source of labour. Initially they worked the sugar cane plantations, while not technically slaves, the indentured servants had very few rights during their terms of indenture. The sugar plantation owners paid their passages to Barbados and expected the servants to work off their debts within three to five years. Though a common practice throughout the 1600s, indentured servitude was viewed as a type of apprenticeship where a poor able-bodied person could work and learn under the support of a sponsor for a specified term.Though almost from the start the indentured servants at the Barbados plantations were treated as little more than slaves. They were at times flogged with cowhide whips. Most of them never complained to the magistrates who were often planters themselves. Whole families were persuaded to sign up particularly those with poor means of income. Those on parish relief were especially vulnerable as often they were stopped it and were forced to sign up. Barbados's labour force was almost wholly enslaved. The slaves in Barbados were forced to work on sugar plantations cutting and processing sugar cane in conditions of severe heat while being subjected to cruel and inhumane treatment, but one of the most physically demanding aspects of sugar production was the grinding of the sugar cane by hand which the slaves were forced to do.

Barbados became one of England's most popular colonies with a rich economy based on sugar and slavery. European slaves had become the main source of labour throughout most of the Barbados island's history. The cultivation of tobacco, cotton, ginger and indigo were initially handled primarily by European indentured labour until the start of the sugar cane industry in the 1640s, which was introduced by Pieter Blower. As mainly the poorest of uneducated labourers were to be recruited in the British Isles and Europe initially to work on the tobacco and cotton plantations. Under the law, these bondservants could not be enslaved but were deemed "tenants at will". They were not permitted to own the land they cultivated or to leave the plantation without permission from their employer. The harsh conditions of this type of servitude gradually made it more difficult for Barbadian tobacco and cotton planters to recruit white labour, hence causing the labour supply to dwindle and the ability of the island's tobacco and cotton producers to compete with their international competitors, to collapse. Richard Ligon, a planter on Barbados from 1647 to 1650, "I have seen an overseer beat a white servant with a cane about the head, till the blood has flowed, for a fault that is not worth the speaking of". But he also noted that planters bought 'servants' in the same way they purchased slaves from Africa, on the very ships that brought them to the island, a process known as 'the scramble'. Both servants and slaves were summoned to the fields early in the morning, often by bells, and they both were worked into the evening. Both were subject to 'severe overseers' who beat them during their labours. Ligon noted that 'I have seen such cruelty there done to servants as I did not think one Christian could have done to another'. If the servants complained, they were beaten again; if they resisted, their period of service (usually from four years to nine years) could be doubled, although terms of service were often ill defined in the case of the Irish. Ligon remembered that so-called servants often found it impossible to 'endure such slavery'.Charles Baily Recalling his time on a Maryland tobacco plantation, he wrote how 'hunger, cold, nakedness, beatings, whippings, and the like … laid many of his fellow labourers … in the dust …I am sure the poor creatures had better have been hanged, than to suffer the death and misery they did'. Having been kidnapped and whipped into work.Between 1627 and 1838 a colonial structure was successfully created based on race and wealth with the economy tied to England, whose impact shaped the islands' society and culture.

In an official Barbados census of 1634, white people numbered about 37,000, while there were 6,000 Afrikan slaves plus an unrecorded number of American Indian women estimated to be a few thousands from the Caribbean and North and South America, who were the wives of English settlers in Barbados. Barbados not only became the most populated of England's overseas colonies, but also one of the most heavily populated colonies in the world. Barbados also played a leading role in the settlement of Jamaica and the Carolinas. During the winter a ship captained by Joseph West with 61 men and women onboard were all destined to be slaves on the Barbados plantations slipped quietly out of Kinsale Harbor in Ireland's coast. But by the time it arrived at its destination in the Caribbean in January 1637, eight of its slave crew were dead. The remaining 53 were sold, including ten to the governor of Barbados himself. All for 450 pounds of sugar apiece. The Captain was instructed to return to London to sell the sugar and then proceed to Kinsale to obtain a fresh cargo of Irish slaves. That initial trickle of white slaves was soon destined to become a torrent of human white slavery.

Slave ship captains were even known to kidnap children from Britain and take them to work on the plantations.During the war of 1637 against the Pequot tribe of North America, orders were given to execute all Pequot men but to take the women and children as prisoners for auctioning in Barbados and other English colonies. Many were burnt alive, and those Pequots who survived the war were enslaved and forced to abandon their Pequot names. The Pequot River was renamed the Thames, and the town of Pequot was changed to New London. British slave traders in the South of

America immediately started slave raids on the Westo and Stono tribes. Then selling the enslaved Native Americans, who were forced to journey by foot to the waiting ships for exportation to Barbados, Antigua, and other ports in the Atlantic regions. Where they were sold as slaves and destined to spend the rest of their lives working for the European colonists. They were sold at Barbados at great financial profit. Whilst local Barbados whites took the women as slaves.

During the years of slavery and colonialism, these different African tribes intermarried among themselves and with the white English slave masters. The Black population also developed qualities that were different to those in the other islands.

There was also an excess of women over men on Barbados which made it different from the other Caribbean islands. Although harsh working conditions were to be expected for indentured servants, the workers on the sugar plantations of Barbados soon found they worked under particularly brutal conditions. Working the cane plantations involved heavy physical labour and very few indentured servants chose to remain as paid labourers once their period of indenture expired. Some did not even live that long, dying before their service ended. With its harsh reputation, finding volunteers for indenture in Barbados became near impossible; The colonists established the Barbadian House of Assembly in 1639. Then in 1642, Barbados planters found a new source of revenue when the Dutch introduced them to sugar cane farming. And by mid 1600's its sugar cane plantations were producing and exporting vast amounts of sugar. The island was attracting wealthy landowners with political affiliations. Enhancing the islands plantocracy, this new emergence of elite planters excluded poor whites and non-whites from Barbados' political infrastructure. The island soon was to gain the largest white population of any of the English colonies in the Americas, thus itself becoming the springboard for English colonisation in the Americas.

In 1645 the young Revd George Downing wrote to his cousin John Winthrop Governor of Connecticut. "If you go to Barbados you shall see a flourishing Island with many able men. I believe that they have bought this year no less than a thousand negroes and the more they buy, the better able are they to buy for, in a year and a half, they will earn (with Gods blessing) as much as they cost".

As sugar developed into the main commercial enterprise, Barbados was divided into large plantation estates that soon replaced the smaller holdings of the early British settlers. The type of weather and soil conditions in Barbados provided the perfect growing conditions for a flourishing sugar industry, and out of this economic experience the Barbados society was created during the mid-1640s, with the changeover to large-scale production and exportation to England. Barbados was desperately in need of slaves to cope with the increased demand for sugar. A planter elite had evolved in Barbados when sugar production soared in the middle of the century and was firmly established there. This elite of English gentlemen and merchants dominated the life of the island for many years, politically, socially and in law. These planters lived a luzorous existence in big houses which were well fornicated and with huge estates, consisting of hundreds of acres each. Many were gamblers fornicators and heavy drinkers. By 1644 over 40 of them held high estates of over 500 acres each. Within each estate was an abundance and variety of servants to wait on their every need, their plantations laboured by slaves and indentured servants flourished and were the norm. Henry Whistler who was himself in servitude in Barbados in 1655 said that "A child born to an enslaved mother was reckoned to be worth £5 Stirling at birth and they grew up with no expense to the masters who sold them as one to the other as we do sheep". Such gentlemen who became planter owners of the plantations estates in the Caribbean were to include the members of the following families, Newton, Drax, Codrington, Ligon. Modyford, Beckfords, Codringtons, Price, Redwoods, Thistlewood, Skeete, Berringer, Clarke, Waldron and the Noel brothers. Barbados was settled by characters who were never over particular about how they made their money. Criminals swiftly became councillors and even pirates. There was an abundance of alcohol on the island although no social norms existed and according and wives, to observers every kind of deviance was recorded, incest, bestiality, sodomy. Normal institutions did not exist there. The church was marginal, judicial systems which had existed in infancy and wives, parents and elders were absent. Theirs was a society of orphans, in which men became almost feral. They formed a new community that was volatile, transient, hyper masculine and intoxicated with its own mythology, that of a land where the young and fearless could build their own paradise. The historian Quaker Richard Pares described these early colonialist as "tough guys, rough unschooled, physically robust men, given to neither self doubt nor rumination". He labelled the islands whites as sinners and he criticised their cruelty towards the indentured slaves reminding them that "they are of the same blood and mould you are of". Henry Whistler wrote of Barbados." This island is the Dunghill whereupon England doth cast forth its rubbish. Rogues and whores and such like people are those which are generally brought here". He concluded.. "a rogue in England will hardly make a cheater here". Many women on the island had been recruited from the London whore houses and prisons. In 1656 Francesco Giavarina the Venetian envoy to Britain claimed that. The soldiers of the London garrison visited various brothels and other places of entertainment where they forcibly laid hands on over 400 women of loose life, whom they compelled to sail for the Barbados islands. Despite their colourful reputations many of these women were powerless desperate, discarded by family, abandoned by husbands, broken by poverty and abuse.

Slaves endured up to 15 hours hard labour daily their work including the cutting of stone and mixing cement. Both torture and executions were common. When the planter John Pinney arrived in Barbados from Dorset in the late 1600s and went to buy slaves in neighbouring St Christopher, he found it an unsettling experience. "I can assure you" he wrote home to a friend, "I was shocked at the first appearance of human flesh exposed to sale". Immediately however he reasons this away. "But surely God ordained them for the use and benefits of us.. otherwise his divine will would have been made manifest by some particular sign or token".The most famous sugar magnet on the island of Barbados was the aristocratic Christopher Codrington. Codrington had built up his profitable estates at Barbados in the early days of the conversion to sugar. His son who was also called Christopher followed in his fathers footsteps. Educated in Britain he became an Oxford scholar On returning to the island he became a councillor and became deputy governor. He later moved to Antigua. When he died in 1710 he was described as the richest and most splendid of all West Indies Grandees. He left his two plantations including their slaves to the Church of England to fund a theological and medical college for young white Barbadian men. Codrington College remains the most noticeable artefact of the golden age of Barbadian sugar.

The young gentlemen, as Courteen called them, many of them alcoholics and certainly none of them were accustomed to hard labour, had no intention of working the land themselves. All visitors remarked on the planters heavy drinking and how insulted inhabitants were if anyone refused their offer of hospitality calling it incivility. Henry Colt who was in Barbados at the time very early lamented the rate of alcohol consumption there and said that to in order to participate in society, he had gone from drinking 2 drams of hot water a meal, to 30 plus in a few days Some said that the planters drank to stimulate their appetites in the heat and because they believed it would help mend their poor digestion,Many of the rich planters were seen to have kept their wives in England. They took their black slaves as their mistresses This procedure was common thus these planters also slept with the off springs, their daughters and their grand daughters. Incest relations was common amongst them. This was one of the main reasons that the planters welcomed Oliver Cromwells Irish slave women. As Cromwell wrote they had only" Negro and Maroon slave women to solace them." ERIC WILLIAMS -From Columbus to Castro 1972.The white indentured labourers were starting to question their place in the future of Barbados' economy during these times. As they were beginning to feel threatened by the increase in African slaves into the island. With no answers and solutions forthcoming they began to leave Barbados in their droves and headed to neighbouring islands. At that time over 30,000 whites migrated to neighbouring islands. This left a racial imbalance that placed the colony's white plantation owners in a weak position. The growing size of the slave labour force with its possibility for rebellion terrified them, but since they were very dependent on the cheap and supposedly infinite stock of African slaves, the colonial officials set about to establish a white supremacy prototype to counter that racial imbalance. There was an uprising in Barbados led by the Irish servants. All of the conspirators were soon arrested and a special Act was passed on 4th October 1649 setting up a council of War for the trial of all those persons guilty of the insurrection. The result of which was that some Eighteen were hanged, drawn and quartered and their heads were set on pikes in prominent positions.In May 1648 240 Welsh single men were sold for a shilling each and shipped to Barbados. European slaves had been the main source of labour during most of the island's history, as poor uneducated labourers were recruited in England, Scotland and Europe to work on the tobacco and cotton plantations. Under the law, these bondservants could not be enslaved but were deemed "tenants at will". They were not permitted to own the land they cultivated or to leave the plantation without permission from their employer. The harsh conditions of this type of servitude gradually made it more difficult for Barbadian tobacco and cotton planters to recruit white labour, hence causing the labour supply to dwindle and the ability of the island's tobacco and cotton producers to compete with their international competitors, to collapse.In the late 1640s and 1650s the popular term to be Barbadosed took on on the more modern meaning or term as Shanghaied. Children were even stolen from their parents and sent to the colony. In Gravesend a ship was found to contain children and servants of several parents and masters so deceived and enticed away, crying and mourning for redemption from their slavery. In 1645 George Downing wrote to John Winthrop, the colonial governor of Massachusetts, stating that planters who wanted to make a fortune in the British West Indies must procure white slave labour "out of England" if they wanted to succeed. Planters came to rely increasingly more on slave labour from West Africa. Barbados attracted more than two-thirds of the number of people from England who emigrated to the "New World". There were around 44,000 settlers living there by 1650 (compared to 12,000 settlers living in Virginia or 23,000 in New England that same year). Rev Aubrey Gynn in the 1930s findings were that probably 50,000 in all were transported to Barbados in the five year period from 1652-1657.The English Civil War was going on during this period and rebels and criminals were transported to Barbados by the civilian Cromwell Puritan government in charge of England at the time. So the vast majority of these "settlers" who were bought to Barbados during this time period were "indentured servants", a few who exchanged five years of labour for their ship's transport fees. But the majority were prisoners of the Cromwellian conquests (1649–53), a portion of the fifty thousand Irish people and the 8,000 predominantly Scottish Royalist prisoners from the Battle of Worcester (1651), sold as indentured labourers under the English Commonwealth regime. Ten thousand were taken prisoner at the battle of Worcester, mainly Scots who were marched to London and 1,500 of them were shipped to Barbados presumably to be sold by auction to the planters there.

For of those persons who were transported during the late 1600s and early 1700s the main reason was due to vagrancy. Gypsies were of course seen as par excellence vagrants. An examination of the lists of those transported found in these works and in the Barbados Records indicated that a great number of individuals bearing Romanichal (British Gypsy) surnames did in fact arrive in Barbados: the names occurring include Boswell, Cook/Cooke, Hern/Herne/Heron, Lee/Leek, Locke, Palmer, Penfold/Pinfold, Price, Scot/Scott, Smith and Ward, ranging from one Pinfold to nine Boswells to over a hundred Smiths. Perhaps only a small percentage of these were likely to have been Gypsies, of course. Sometimes, a further clue was provided by the county of origin of the individual, where given (Cookes from Middlesex and Kent), or by occupation (Boswell), a blacIn March of 1650. Richard and Barbara Smith and with Francis and Elizabeth Parker along with Elizabeth Grey were taken to York Castle dungeons and no doubt executed obviously for being Gypsies and similar minor offences. ksmith), but these must also be considered non-conclusive.A letter dated 1654 written by Thomas Herbert clerk of Council Dublin castle to the governor of Barbados Daniel Searle stated "His highness and Council for the affairs of Ireland have ordered Captain Jon Norris to take aboard his ship divers Irish man and women such as are found by the Justices to be vagabonds and idlers. to be exported to the Barbados or some other the English plantation Islands of the Cariba or thereabouts". In 1661 'Commissions and Instructions' were issued anew to justices and constables, by Act o f Parliament, with the view of arresting Gypsies. A great many Gypsies were no doubt deported to the British 'plantations' in Virginia, Jamaica and Barbados during the second half of the seventeenth century. That they had there to undergo a temporary, if not 'perpetual' servitude, seems very likely (MacRitchie, 1894:102).Barbados was to become the transportation destination for a wide range of military prisoners, Irish natives and British vagrants in the early years of the colony's growth. Cromwell had exploited the island as a place of exile for Scotch and Irish prisoners of war, as well as for rebellious men. Taken from the streets of Ireland for shipment to Barbados as slaves. Cromwell and king James had sent thousands to servitude into Barbados and the other West Indies plantations thousands of men, women and children. The plantations had needed more labour than the surviving Ameridian Indians could provide. So that the European workers were used as a source of plantation labour for all of the British colonies such as Barbados. So that soon as well as the Indentured servants, political prisoners (both Irish and English) and common criminals were brought in to add to the Barbados labour force.

The English traffic in slaves in the first half of the seventeenth century was in White slavery. Cromwell issued his new policy of pardons to criminals providing that they go overseas. This greatly increased the numbers coming to Barbados particularly of felons committed to death, sturdy beggers, along with Gypsies who were regarded as vagrants and other troublesome rogues, poor and idle debauched persons. As a consequence some 400 lady prostitutes were also shipped to Barbados in 1656 from the London brothels. Though this was in order through their breeding with the populace that they would replenish the white Barbados population. All of these prisoners and newcomers were treated very cruelly. As one account tells us that. "On the ship the prisoners were kept below decks for nearly three weeks at Plymouth, during the six weeks voyage to Barbados they were all locked up under decks amongst the horses". "On their arrival on the island they were sold". "The generality of them to most inhuman and barbarous persons, and then set to work grinding at the mills, attending the furnaces and then digging in the scorching heat. They were it is clear the chattels of their masters and bought and sold still from one planter to another, whipped at the whipping post for their masters pleasure, and many ways made miserable beyond expression of Christian imagination".From the middle of the 1600s onward, planters began to purchase ever more enslaved workers to supplement and, eventually, to replace indentured labourers. The slaves in Barbados were forced to work on sugar plantations cutting and processing sugar cane in conditions of severe heat while being subjected to cruel and inhumane treatment.Barbados served as a main point of recess as an entrepôt for the distribution of slaves to other British territories in the western hemisphere for many years. Whether ultimately bound for Virginia, Jamaica or elsewhere, large numbers of slaves passed first of all through that island (Hancock, 1980b). There was also an excess of women over men in both racial groups, a pattern which surfaced in the last decades of the 17th century that made Barbados different to the other Caribbean islands where the reverse was the case in both racial groups. A visitor in 1651 wrote that "servants served for four years, at the moment of freedom, the servant was supposed to receive, which he had clearly earned £10 Stirling, or the value of it in goods". The writer added sardonically "if his master be so honest as to pay it". The implication was that dishonest masters could get by with sending servants away to fend for themselves with nothing. One Coole having robbed the post and so condemned to be hanged, would not accept of a reprieve, but rather would chose to be executed than to be sent to Barbados.

Barbados had become the largest sugar producer in the Caribbean. Barbadian planters were also well aware that the island had an increasing sugar production compared to the other islands and newly gained territories. By 1667 it became such a strategic and well known centre for Amerindian slavery in the Caribbean that its numbers of slaves onto the islands plantations had increased substantially from 6,000 in 1645 to 80,000.During these years there were (3) unsuccessful slave rebellions in Barbados; 1649, 1675 and 1692. The First Slave Rebellion was in 1649 this included two plantations the trigger was insufficient food. It was quickly subdued with not much damage. The Second Slave Rebellion was in 1675.This one was island-wide and took over three years to plan but was uncovered when a one of the slaves named Fortuna leaked the information out. Over 100 slaves were arrested and tortured, while over 40 were executed after being found guilty of rebellion. Some committed suicide before being executed, while others were beheaded or burnt alive. The Third Slave Rebellion was in 1692. This was also island-wide with over 200 slaves arrested and over 90 executed after being found guilty of rebellion.

The white slaves and indentured labourers on Barbados were known as "redlegs".No doubt this was a reference to the sunburn they were prone to in the hot tropical sun. Their descendants still live on the island. In 1689, the governor of Barbados, Colonel James Kendall, described the Red legs as being "dominated over and used like dogs." He suggested to the local assembly that the emancipated slaves be given two acres (0.8 hectares) of land, as was their due, but the assembly contemptuously turned down the request. Today, their descendants are still there, adding to the rich culture of Barbados. However, minute books from the island show that no more than a fifth of those who were freed became farmers, owners, or artisans. The remainder of the workers formed a wretched, poor and isolated community known as red legs.In 1674 Captain Peter Wroth sailed from Barbados on his ship *the Savoy* for the Dutch Guiana coastline in South America with a legal order from the Barbados English Governor Lord Willoughby and Sir Peter Colleton, "to capture Arawak Indians for sale in Barbados". A year later, 160 Wampanoag Indians were captured in the U.S.A. and sent to Barbados to be sold and traded for Afrikan slaves. Among these 160 Wampanoags was a distinguished Chief Metacomet (also known as King Philip), along with his wife Nanuskooke and their only son of 9 years, who were all sold into slavery in Barbados for one pound sterling each to a local English planter. In all, there were 900 Wampanoag Indians that were sold as slaves in Barbados.The Spanish Governor of Florida in 1682 recorded that "The English of South Carolina were capturing Native Florida Indians from the Spanish missions to be sold as slaves in the island of Barbados". Early plantation deeds in Barbados confirm that American Indian slaves with Spanish names were arriving in Barbados during this time British slave traders in the South of America operated out of Charles Town renamed Charleston, a city founded by them in South Carolina. They immediately started slave raids on the Westo and Stono tribes, engaging in the thriving business of selling enslaved Native Americans, who were forced to journey by foot from the remote regions. Where they were captured and taken to the waiting ships for exportation to Barbados, Antigua, and other ports in the Atlantic regions for sale. Where they would spend the rest of their lives as slaves working for the European colonists.

These captives were sold or traded in Barbados at great financial profit, with local whites taking the women as wives and concubines, while they traded the men for Afrikan slaves. Some 900 Wampanoag Indians were sold as slaves in Barbados. The almost white skinned Susquehannock Indians were extradited to Barbados, Bequia and Bimini.

King James 2nd and George 2 had used Barbados to get rid of the Monmouth rebels and followers of Prince Charles, since the rebel James Scott, the first Duke of Monmouth, attempted to seize the English throne from his uncle the Duke of York who had become King of England, Scotland, and Ireland upon the death of his older brother Charles 2nd on February 6th 1685.

Thousands of people had taken part in the Monmouth Rebellion which started in Dorset England against King James. The trials for treason were conducted by Judge Jeffries in his position as the chief Justice, at his court in Dorchester. He listened to the cases of the rebels captured after the collapse of Monmouth's Rebellion. This was known as the Bloody Assizes, he had tried 500 people a day from thousands taken prisoner. Of these hundreds were sentenced its estimated that 200-300 persons were hanged. Hundreds were fined, flogged, or imprisoned and were whipped throughout all the towns in Dorset. Including Weymouths youth William Wiseman, aged just 14 years. His crime was to read the proclamation of Monmouth in the town.Due to the large numbers sentenced and hung, Judge Jeffries was to gain notoriety as The Hanging Judge. Over 800 of the convicted prisoners were transported as slaves on the long journey to Barbados. Sailing on two slave ships these were the ship *'Happy Return'* of Poole and the *'Betty'* of London which sailed from Weymouth in Dorset to Barbados. They were destined to work as slaves on the sugar plantations. Only around 600 of them survived the journey in the appalling conditions to Barbados but of these they were to be granted a free pardon in 1691.The light regard paid to the personal right of individuals was shown by a wholesale deportation of poor people at this time to the West Indies ... out of a desire as well to promote the Scottish and English plantations in Jamaica and Barbados for the honour of their country, as to free the kingdom of the burden of many strong and idle beggars, Egyptians, common and notorious thieves, and other dissolute and loose persons banished and stigmatised for gross crimes (Chambers, 1858:304). Barbados was regarded as one of the leaders in the Slave trade from the European Territories, playing a vital role in the early buying and selling of Africans, which connected the Caribbean to West Africa and England.

In 1691, the first law relating solely to slavery was passed, and remained in operation for about 20 years. The Assembly passed an all-inclusive law for slaves, and the majority of the terminology was adopted from the Barbados Slave Code of 1688. The constant importation of slaves was caused by the high mortality rate, due to bad conditions and overwork. By the 1700's, Barbados was one of the leaders in the slave trade from the European colonies.It appears that many of the Gypsies on Barbados were treated far more cruelly than at any of the other British colonies. For as one observer politician Major General Tottenham admitted when addressing Parliament that from what he had witnessed on the island that this was unfortunately the case. At the time he quoted an African slave who was made to wear a collar with spikes which prevented him from being able to sit or lie down. With his body being covered in sores.In the colonies the best prices were paid for such good breeding stock amongst the traders. This was particularly so at one time when Negro men outnumbered women four to one. As a result of which Gypsy women were more likely to become slaves particularly for the Caribbean slave market specifically destined for sexual relationships with the mainly black slaves at Barbados. Particularly young attractive Gypsy women were essential for breeding purposes to obtain future generations of slaves. This was particularly so in Barbados where young attractive. full breasted white women were preferred to any other slaves at that time.Colonel A. B.Ellis stated in an article later in 1883 "Few but readers of old Colonial papers and records are aware that a lively trade was carried out between England and the plantations as the colonies were then called from 1647 to 1690, in political prisoners, where they were sold to the colonialists for various terms of years, sometimes for Life"

CHAPTER NINE

CARIBBEAN DAYS

Caribbean Conquests

On the Caribbean conquests its like riding on the waves
with his cutlass drawn for battles
and his over boards and slaves
with his flag still flying high with jolly roger fame
he rides the seven seas till he See's land again

Oh the pirates and their parrots
have all sailed from the bays
where the salty foams still rising
from the charter miles sway

When the boy up in the nest box
yells land upon the shore
you've gotta count your blessings
that its a foreign shore

There's bullion's in the galleons
and gold to deck the land
with cannons firing daily and a pirate loyal band
there's a view to set the hearts a racing
and a spyglass set to see
all the seven wonders
from the seven roaring seas

The cabin boy was crying
and the wench was sleeping free
with virgin flesh awaiting him
and a road to victory

There's a tavern some where waiting
and rum to fit to pour
with seven gorgeous virgins
awaiting on the shores

Ray Wills

Barbados was the Jewel in the Crown of the British Empire. For 200 years after 1650 the West Indies were the most fought-over colonies in the world, as Europeans made and lost immense fortunes growing and trading in sugar- a commodity so lucrative that it was known as white gold. Young men, beset by death and disease, an ocean away from the moral anchors of life in Britain, created immense dynastic wealth but produced a society poisoned by war, sickness, cruelty and corruption. The Sugar Barons explores the lives and experiences of those whose fortunes rose and fell with the West Indian empire. From the ambitious and brilliant entrepreneurs, to the grandees wielding power across the Atlantic, to the inheritors often consumed by decadence, disgrace and madness, this is the compelling story of how a few small islands and a handful of families decisively shaped the British Empire. By the early 1700s Barbados was in close competition for Brazil in the world sugar market. The combination of Jewish finance and White slave labour had made it the richest colony in the British Empire. The island's value, in terms of trade and capital exceeded that of all other British colonies combined. (John Oldmixon, The British Empire in America, vol. 2, p. 186.)From from the beginning of the 1700s, the majority of Black Barbadians were born locally. This large proportion of locally born Blacks of African descent as opposed to imported Afrikans, was to contribute greatly to the early development of the Barbadian identity. The wealth of Barbados was founded on the backs of White slave labour there can be no doubt. White slave labourers from Barbados.In 1714, British merchants and planters applied to the Privy Council for permission to ship Gypsies to the Caribbean, avowedly to be used as slaves (MacRitchie, op. cit.), During the 1700's to the 1800's, Barbados shifted from a majority white population to majority black. This caused tension on the island as white indentured servants became unsure of their place, and plantation owners were afraid of slave rebellion, eventually causing most of them to leave. Although quite small, there were some freed slaves most of whom worked as tradesmen but could not vote. Because of racial discrimination many freed slaves tended to gravitate towards the British culture and its white supremacy to fit in, separating themselves from other slaves.In January 1st, 1715, Prisoners were sentenced to be transported to the plantations for being [by] habit and repute gipsies. On the said gipsies coming here the town was brought under a burden [and] they had used endeavours with several merchants who have ships now going abroad [i.e., to transport them as slaves], for which they are to receive thirteen pounds sterling (Memorabilia, 1835:424-426). Among the family names of those individuals were Faa, Fenwick, Lindsey, Stirling, Robertson, Ross and Yorstoun.. British ports outfitted nearly one-third of all transatlantic slave voyages, transporting almost one million Africans to Jamaica and almost half a million to the small island of Barbados before ruling the trade illegal in 1807.The South Carolina code described any Negro, Mulatto or Indian who had been bought or sold was to be labelled a slave, and this classification was also to be extended to the offspring of these slaves. The Barbados slave codes became the model on which every other British Caribbean colony in the West Indies was patterned. These codes created harsh slave laws, gang labour for Africans along with a 12 hour work day, and barbaric punishment for violations of the slave laws.

The Barbados slaves were forced to work on sugar plantations cutting and processing sugar cane in conditions of severe heat while being subjected to cruel and inhumane treatment, but one of the most physically demanding aspects of sugar production was the grinding of the sugar cane by hand which the slaves were forced to do. Barbados became one of England's most popular colonies with a rich economy based on sugar and slavery. By the mid-1700s most slaves were free, their places taken by Africans.The white slave trade became a very profitable venture. For an Irish white slave could be sold in Barbados for between £10 and £35 a head. The English traffic in slaves in the early 1600s had been solely in White slaves. The Irish slave trade had been initially set into motion when James 2nd sold 30,000 Irish prisoners as slaves to the New World. For a decree issued earlier in 1625 mandated that Irish political prisoners be transported overseas and sold to English settlers in the West Indies. Ireland rapidly became the biggest supplier of human cattle for English merchants,In his book published in 1903 Dr Thomas Addis eminent historian stated that" Over one hundred thousand young children who were orphans had been taken from their Irish Catholic parents were sent abroad into slavery in the West Indies, Virginia and New England". The slave ships departed from Bristol and London included *the Jane*, *The Swan* and *Mary*, *The Elizabeth* and *The Two Brothers*. By 1720 there were nearly 150 British ships engaged in the slave trade, mostly from London and Bristol, but also Liverpool and lesser ports. During the following decade, the British shipped more than 100,000 enslaved Africans to the America, about a tenth of whom ended up in the North American mainland colonies, and a great number in Cuba. But the British English Caribbean also maintained a similarly inexhaustible demand for new slaves.

Barbados was regarded as one of the leaders in the Slave trade from the European Territories, playing a vital role in the early buying and selling of Africans, which connected the Caribbean to West Africa and England.In 1739, the Barbados Parliament authorized legislation that allowed slaves to give evidence against the three categories of non-white people living in Barbados, freed Negroes, Amerindians, and Mulattos - who were accepted as mixtures of white and Negro, white and Amerindian or Negro and Amerindian.Barbadian law banned slaves from leaving their plantations without permission from their owners, and also prevented them from beating drums, blowing horns, or playing other loud instruments, because this was seen as a medium that allowed those slaves who spoke different languages to be able to communicate with each other. Other authorized restrictions broadened this objective by outlawing parties on Sundays, which was the Christian day of rest. Barbados passed its own adaptation of the Fugitive Slave Law, which required all whites to return runaway slaves to colonial officials. This law was however relaxed when it came to a slave master who deliberately killed a slave, requiring him to pay only a $15 fine, but those who killed their slaves"accidentally" usually escaped without being fined.

In 1751, George Washington, then 19 years old, came to Barbados with his brother Lawrence to recuperate from tuberculosis. while in Barbados, he contracted smallpox. Provided with excellent care, he quickly recovered and his body built up a natural immunity to the virus. This became important later when his army was decimated by smallpox during the American war of independence, but the immune Washington was not affected and survived to win the war, later becoming the first president of the U.S.A.

Colonel John Scott wrote of his experiences on the Island he described black and white slaves working together there side by side."They are just permitted to live and a very great part Irish, derided by the negros and branded with the Epither of white slaves... He wrote I have from my particular satisfaction inspected many of their Plantations, and have seen 30,sometimes 40,Christians, English, Scotch and Irish at work in the parching sun without shirt, shoe or stocking"."Barbados had a tumultuous history and a painful legacy. Older folks there remember the days when British royalty would visit. They would stand in the sun waving the union flag, hoping to catch a glimpse of the Queen or her representatives. But Little England has grown up, it has matured, it should no longer be loitering in its "master's castle"

- Prof Hilary Beckles.

Barbadian planters recognised that the island had an increasing slave population that would guarantee continuous sugar production, while the other regions such as the newly occupied territories like Trinidad, Essequibo, Demerara and Berbice (Guyana), would be hampered in their economic development if access to slave labour was denied.The colony had its own share of problems which included raids by Spanish and French pirates, in addition to chaotic weather that decimated crops and triggered African and Irish slave revolts. These revolts often coincided with the raids and uncontrollable weather which distracted the slave owners, who would send slaves to other settlers or towns for help. The freedom to move around gave slaves the opportunity to convey information to other revolutionaries. These rebellions increased the fear of white slave owners.

Towards the end of the 1700s the younger Pitt estimated that four fifths of the wealth of the British incomes derived from overseas came from the West Indies. Jamaica was described as a constant mine whence Britain draws prodigious Riches and as a necessary appendage to our present refined manner of living. Sugar was king imports from Barbados had quadrupled they had trebled between 1700 to 1740 and doubled since. Barbados passed its own adaptation of the Fugitive Slave Law, which required all whites to return runaway slaves to colonial officials. This law was however relaxed when it came to a slave master who deliberately killed a slave, requiring him to pay only a $15 fine, but those who killed their slaves"accidentally"usually escaped without being fined. The Barbados slave codes became the model on which every other British Caribbean colony in the West Indies was patterned, including Jamaica and Antigua who passed identical laws in 1664 and 1702. These promoted harsh slave laws, gang labour for Africans with a 12 hour work day, and barbaric punishment for violations of the slave laws. Barbadian law banned slaves during the mid-eighteenth century from leaving their plantations without permission from their owners, and also prevented them from beating drums, blowing horns, or playing other loud instruments, because this was seen as a medium that allowed those slaves who spoke different languages to be able to communicate with each other. Other authorized restrictions broadened this objective by outlawing parties on Sundays, which was the Christian day of rest. The planters of Barbados are cruel to their unhappy slaves, who are condemned to servile labour and scanty fare. Wrote a Rhode islander, John Benson in the 1760s. Benson was shocked to see the heads of slaves, fixed upon sharp pointed stakes, while their unburied carcases were exposed to be torn by dogs and vultures on the sandy beach. In 1803 war broke out with the Spanish and French combining forces against Britain. Admiral Nelson in 1805 wrote to Lord Seaforth, the Governor of Barbados, "Your Lordship may rely that everything in my power shall be done to preserve the colonies".

Lieutenant Edward Thompson would be shocked to see witness to the habitual extreme violence.-whippings and executions-used at that time to enforce discipline in the royal navy, but he was still deeply shocked to see in Barbados which he pronounced kinder than the other islands a young slave girl tortured to death for some trivial domestic error. Thompson ascribed to cruelty to the way the

Barbadians were taught in their very infancy to flog with a whip the slave that offends them.

By the 1800s the elite wealthy British plantation owners were building elaborate estates like Drax Hall and St. Nicholas Abbey, which still exist, while controlling the House of Assembly and the Legislative Council. They encouraged slave reproduction to avoid more importations of slaves, becoming the only island in the British Caribbean no longer dependent on slave imports. The majority of blacks in Barbados were born locally, with a high percentage of Creole born blacks, as opposed to Africans. This enabled the black population to reproduce itself, rather than rely on new imports from Africa to maintain population levels.

In 1807 the International Slave Trade was abolished giving slaves in Barbados hope of freedom, but abolitionist missionaries and antislavery debates seemed to hinder the process, ultimately causing the 1816 Revolt by Bussa of Bayley's Plantation. Bussa is now one of Barbados' National heroes with the Emancipation statute being erected in his memory.Rebellions of the slave populations simmered in Barbados until 1816 due to an increase in free blacks and slaves born on the island (these were called Creole Slaves), there were also more frequent visits to the island by British Military Ships for supplies and a colonial militia which was becoming more powerful during the 1800's.

Creole Slaves were believed to be more submissive than African born slave and therefore were placed over the Africans. Then during the 1816 rebellion more than 800 slaves were killed while fighting and over 100 executed. This was the first rebellion of this size in Barbados and the Caribbean, and took part for (3) days on the southern part of the island. This rebellion caused reform to ease the hardships of slavery. The laws regulating the slaves were strongly enforced by the 1800's, when there were laws prohibiting slaves from leaving their plantations without permission and stopping them from beating drums or any other instruments used by slaves to communicate with each other. There were also laws requiring the return of runaway slaves and leniency for those killing slaves.

As the cost of white labour rose in England, more slaves were imported from West Africa, especially the Gold Coast and by extension more black slaves were brought to Barbados. The main groups of slaves imported were from Ibibio, Yoruba, Lgbo and Efik, as well as Asante, Fante, Ga and Fon. By mid 1600's there was over 5600 black African slaves in Barbados and by early 1800,s over 385,000.In 1825 the 'Amelioration Policy' was changed to 'the Consolidated Slave Law' legislation (The Emancipation Act) which consist of (3) Rights for Slaves; The right to own property / The right to testify in all court cases / Reduction of fees charged for Manumission (a fee charged to slave owners for emancipating their slaves). The British abolished slavery in 1833. This act emancipated the Irish slaves in the British West Indies. By 1834 slavery was abolished in all the territories of British rule. This was mainly due to the Consolidated Slave Law (The emancipation Act) and (3) major uprisings; Bussa Rebellion (Barbados- 1816) / Demerara Revolt (now Guyana- 1823) / Jamaica Revolt (1832). Because of the instability within the Caribbean, the British Parliament was forced to emancipate over 80,000 slaves at this time. Enslaved Africans worked on the Sugar plantations established on the Island until 1834 when Slavery was abolished.

The British planters received substantial finacial compensation from the British government to offset their losses from labour for their estates and plantations through the new slavery bill.

Those planter families who obtained compensation from the British government for loss of earnings from Slavery in the families sugar plantations in the West Indies included William Pinney MP for Lyme Regis Dorset from 1832. He received in excess of £30,000 in compensation when slavery was abolished in 1834. The freed slaves however never received a penny.

In 1838 the Masters and Servant Act (Contract Law) made discrimination against persons of colour in Barbados illegal. Although slavery was abolished. None of this freed people such as the Irish to the degree they wanted because America had classified them as 'coloured' and treated them accordingly. It was only after the ruling class accepted them as 'white' that they could finally say: "I'm free, white and 21."

Apprenticeships for freed slaves were then introduced under labour contracts as indentured servants. In Barbados Indentured Servants could not join the islands educational systems, and labour contracts were for (12) years, making it the longest in the Caribbean, as well as being paid the lowest wages in the region. Some worked (45) hour weeks without pay in exchange for accommodations in tiny huts. As the increased production and demand for sugar gained pace, more workers were required. Africans had been used as workers on Spanish and Portugese islands like Madeira in the Atlantic Ocean. They were valued as agricultural workers. Gradually, more and more enslaved peoples from Africa were captured, sold, and brought across the Atlantic Ocean to work on the plantations. Africans were well equipped to deal with the hot climate, had developed immunities to European diseases and were used to agricultural work.

- Robert Dawson

George Fox who founded the Quakers preached abolition in Barbados but was himself the owner of slaves in a colony in Pennsylvania. In 1805 Jamaica was the biggest producer of sugar in the world producing nearly 100,000 tons. It was the future king of England William 1V who as Duke of Clarence led the opposition in the house of Lords to William Wilberforces Abolition of Slavery. Wilberforce talked of child slaves from Bristol being sold to Ireland in the reign of Henry V11.

CHAPTER TEN

THE DRAX HALL ESTATE

Plantation Gentlemen

All the English gentlemen
who sailed upon the seas
with all their fine clothes
and their merchant ships

They spoke of liberty
their adventurous spirit
and their speech was rich
for all to hear and see

For the ships they sailed
were rich in trade so free
whilst their captives lived below
with their shackled loins
and chains of slavery

They sailed to pastures new
where sugar cane and fields of hope
awaited for their toil
on golden sands
where the greed of man
built up their rich estates

Midst Caribbean shifts and seawards drifts
they made their masters rich
the gentlemen of English lanes
took to the task with pride
whilst their slaves they toiled with little joy
and great men grew to fame

With Baron jests and palaces
they lived a life of ease
their coffee house meets
and fortunes gained

Far from their English country lanes
their fortunes were achieved
where gentleman and poor alike
lived their lives beneath the setting sun

Ray Wills

On 16th February 1627 two young British merchants James and William Drax had sailed to Barbados. James was just 18 years of age. They sailed alongside other young adventurers and future planters Holdip and Hillard. On board the ship *William and John,* which was commanded by Henry Powell who was the brother of John Powell and commissioned by the wealthy Courteens. It was the first slavers vessel despatched to Barbados and as well as produce and commodities carried some 50 settlers in all. Shortly after it was to ferry scores more settlers with dreams of a good life in Barbados. Holdip a planter alongside Drax told the story of how he and Drax had roughed it on the island in the early days living at first in a cave in the rocks prior to building primitive shelters for themselves out of sticks. How they cleared lush land in the centre of the island and eventually took on the task of growing and processing sugar. After flirting with an unsuccessful tobacco crop. Then later shipping the crop to England making a healthy profit. It was a large enough sum at the time for him to buy forty to fifty indentured servants to work the land for him. Over time they devised a commercial sugar plantation model, which was worked by slaves. Later according to Ligon, "Drax beginning on the island was founded on a stock not exceeding £300 Stirling, has raised his fortune to such a height, As I have heard him say, that "he would not look towards England, with the purpose to remain there the rest of his life, till he were able to purchase an estate of ten thousand pounds land yearly, which he hoped to in a few years to accomplish, with what he was then owner of, and all by this plant of sugar".By the mid 1630s Drax, a Commissioner for roads and a captain in the militia had become a leading light in this infant colony and the success story of his family. He had married Meliora Horton from Somerset who was most likely related to him and his brother Williams wife Ursula. By then James and his brother had gone into a partnership with a Thomas Middleton. Meliora and James first child also James was born around 1639 and their second child Henry was born in 1641. Colonel James Drax became one of the richest and influential men on Barbados. Ending up with a knighthood from Cromwell thus becoming Sir James Drax and a Baron from the King whilst marrying the Earl of of Carlisles daughter. From 1642 Sir James Drax had become the second man

135

to cultivate sugar cane in the Caribbean. The first being Colonel James Holdip but as an account in 1667 stated the Colonels efforts failed to produce any success. By the mid 1640s Drax and Hilliard were in possession of great estates on the island though the land they owned was still very much in a state of being worked on before it was fully at its best. Drax was the first to build a factory in the field and most likely Hilliard also processed his sugar there too. Drax increased his slave holdings by the purchase of 34 of the 254 slaves on board the slave ship *Mary Bonaventure*. In the same year he built the islands first windmill. Drax, an early account maintains, had imported from Holland the model of a sugar mill for the crushing of the canes to extract to extract te juice, and some copper cauldrons for boiling the liquid until it was ready to crystallise. With his Drax hall plantation it was the result of his ingenuity to perfect a Dutch technique for processing sugar which established the Drax family fortune. However, as stated by Matthew Parker, "James Drax holds the distinct dishonour of being seemingly the first, or among the first, to convert from using indentured labour- where the worker works off a debt and then goes free- to enslaved labour- where the worker works for nothing, has no rights, and is never free". He was in later years described as an ingenious spirit he was certainly that. Whilst taken all this on he had forged strong links with sugar traders and later through them Jewish traders based in Amsterdam the capital of sugar refining in the world. He was no doubt very ambitious as well as very well connected and willing to learn. According to a friend of Drax, bringing the business of growing sugar and its processing during the 1640s took diverse years pains, care, patience and industry, with the disbersing of vast amounts of money. By 1650 Drax Hall estate belonging to the Draxs had become one of largest of the slave plantation estates at Barbados it contains 879-acres. In his History of Barbados. Sir Richard Schomburg wrote of Sir James Drax and his life at Drax Hall Barbados: "He appears to have lived in great style": Richard Ligon tells us "he fared like a prince, and killed now and then an ox". In the summer of 1661 James Drax aged 52 took ill and died. It was the end of a life characterised by energy, perseverance and wide ranging talent, which aided by good fortune and excellent contacts, had transformed not only Barbados but the entire Atlantic word. His son James aged 22 took on the family business but from London. He led a fast life of wine and women then died in in his 24th year. In the late 1660s Henry Drax wife Frances had died and in July 1671 whilst on council business in England Henry had remarried to Dorothy Lovelace who was the daughter of Lord John Lovelace. In 1669 Sir James Drax brother, William Drax, had taken the art of sugar processing to Jamaica and his brother-in-law, estate owner Colonel Christopher Codrington, took it to Antigua. Henry Drax the second son of the original James Drax then became owner of the Barbados estate in 1680. He was at that time said to be the wealthiest planter in 17th century Barbados.John Oldmixon (1673-1742) asserts that "Colonel Drax, from a stock of £300, raised the greatest estate of any planter of his time, except for Richard Walter." (1636-1700), John Samuel Wanley Sawbridge was the eldest son of Samuel Elias Sawbridge (b.1769- d.1851), an MP and landowner, and the grandson of John Sawbridge (1732?-1795), MP for Hythe 1768-74 and for London 1774-1795 and Lord Mayor of London in 1775. In 1827 he married Jane, the daughter of Richard Erle-Drax Grosvenor and a member of the Drax family which was so prominent among the slave-owners of Barbados. On the marriage, Sawbridge assumed the name of Erle-Drax.

The MP for the nearby borough of Wareham, Dorset, A captain in the East Kent Militia; had raised a troop of the Dorset shire Yeomanry in 1830 to deal with the Swing Riots; He was patron of five church livings; appointed sheriff of Dorset, January 1840; a deputy-lieutenant of Dorset in the late 1850s.Historian Hilary Beckle estimated that close to 30,000 enslaved men, women and children had died on the Drax Caribbean plantations over 200 years. By 1832 there were 275 people enslaved on the plantations producing 300 tons of sugar and 140 puncheons of rum. The Drax families slave plantations in Jamaica were sold in the mid-1800s. The Barbados plantation was worked by up to 327 slaves at a time, with the death rate for both adults and children high. Sir Hilary Beckles, chairman of the 20-state Caribbean Community's (Caricom) Reparations Commission and vice-chancellor of the University of the West Indies, estimates that as many 30,000 slaves died on the Drax plantations in Barbados and Jamaica over 200 years. In 1833 around £20m was then paid out to compensate slave owners. A database created by University College London showed that Richard Drax's ancestor John Sawbridge Erle-Drax MP, who also lived at Charborough Park, received £4,293 12s 6d – a very large sum in 1836 – in compensation for freeing 189 slaves. Official sources in Barbados confirm that Richard's father owned the plantation and had passed it on to his oldest son, Richard. Official documentation shows the MP now controls Drax Hall Plantation.Harvested sugar cane is no longer processed at the plantations but taken to a central processing plant and then refined for export."historically "the Drax family has done more harm and violence to the black people of Barbados than any other family. The Draxes built and designed and structured slavery". Beckles- David Commissioning, Barbados's ambassador to Caricom, says of the Drax family: "You can't simply walk away from the scene of the crime. They have a responsibility now to make some effort to help repair the damage". By 1834, (two years before slavery was abolished), the Drax Hall estate had 189-slaves working its 879-acres estate. Between 1825 and 1834, its estate produced an average of 163-metric tons of sugar and 4,845-gallons of rum per year. Although now refined elsewhere, the Drax Hall plantation still harvests sugar and it is still owned by- though not home to- the Drax family. Drax hall sugar plantation has now remained in the Drax family for over 3 centuries. It is the oldest plantation and the largest in Barbados with some 800 acres. During which time the Drax family owners were said to have imposed countless cruelties on enslaved peoples. The Drax's Caribbean slave plantations and estates then descended with that of Charleborough House in Dorset. Drax Plantation still looks very much like a plantation might look back in the 17th century. A plantation like this could be used to help teach us about our history. The Erle family had owned Charborough House, Dorset, since the 16th Century and through the marriage, Drax took possession of it. On his family's side he inherited Olantigh, near Wye, Kent in 1851. He is said to have 'spent money prodigiously' [Matthew Beckett] on both Olantigh and Charborough Park. Including the building of the distinctive celebrated brick wall surrounding the estate which is said to use well in excess of some 2 million bricks from local brickworks.

Whilst at Olantigh, large picture galleries and collections of art, Venetian Towers and garden ornaments, such as a huge fountain at the entrance, were added.Following Draxs death in 1887 the house and estate at Olantigh passed to his nephew, Wanley Ellis Sawbridge-Erle-Drax, who spent his time between Charborough in Dorset and Olantigh, until 1903 when the house burnt down. He also owned an estate at Holnest, Dorset where he built an elaborate mausoleum besides the parish church which was demolished in 1935 and replaced by a flat memorial stone. The Sawbridge and Erle-Drax families had a number of estates in the counties of Dorset, Wiltshire, Somerset, Yorkshire (including Ellerton Abbey), Lincolnshire, Surrey, Suffolk as well as Drax hall in Barbados.Drax Hall in Barbados remains an important investment. Its present owner and of all the Drax family estates is British MP Richard Drax (aka Richard Grosvenor Plunkett- Ernle-Erle- Drax, M.P.),Today Drax Hall is worth an estimated £4.7 million and Richard Drax's total inherited wealth is estimated at £150-million. Today most consider that the Drax family owe a debt of gratitude to the slaves and the country that has given them nearly four centuries-worth of vast wealth and unbridled privilege. It is then a rather sad legacy that the only reason most people have ever heard of their distinctive name is not because of even just one endowment, but because of a villain in a James Bond movie. Whilst in Dorset England Richard Drax lives the traditional life all the trappings of an aristocratic country gentleman similar to the landed gentry of an earlier age. All the trappings are there, the military, hunting, shooting and farming.

THE GREAT WALL OF DORSET

After cycling for sometime through narrow hedgegrow lanes. I found myself cycling on a very long stretch of a road . To my left views of meadows and to my right was a long and high brick wall which seemed to go on forever here in the heart of Dorset on the A31 there is a high brick wall butted up tight to the road that seems to go on for ever. This"great wall of Dorset" shields Charborough Park from the outside world.. I knew from my own readings that this was built by French prisoners of war in the Napoleonic war.Then i reached the end of the wall the familiar high stone entrance pillars of the Drax estate. With its majestic distinctive five legged antlered stag deer proudly displayed on the top of its pillars. This was the boundary wall estate of the famed wealthy landlord Drax .Where rumour had it that the lord Drax could only see three legs of the deer from his manor house. This didnt please him and it was said that he had them craft an extra leg. So he could view the normal four legs of the stag. It was said that he had made his great wealth by means of the slave trade. Along with his many foreign plantations in far away places such as the Drax hall estate Barbados.After studying the wall and the entrance pillars for a while I got back on my bike and continued the journey. I wondered if the hard dark red bricks of the wall were all built by the slave labour of local gypsy brick makers and laborers sweat. I wondered how many brickyards did Drax have in those days. And how many poor young men worked these pits and mannings to meet his requirements. The number of bricks used on the wall surrounding the Drax estate must have been gone into thousands upon thousands. These poor souls no doubt worked for years to create these bricks for his wall. I was aware that there were three brickyards in Bere alone but there were many more in the area and these bricks were all of local dark red clay. All those bricks wasted on a wall when they could have been used to house hundreds of folk. Reminds me of one of these modern day popularist politicans whose chant was "build that wall".

-Extract from my novel, *The Time Traveller.*

Drax Charborough house is home to Richard Grosvenor Plunkett-Ernle-Erle- Drax. Richard is the Conservative MP for South Dorset, who lives in the palatial Grade I-listed mansion, hidden from public view within the 700-acre private grounds. The Park, with its outstanding garden and ancient deer park, is just a part of the 14,000 acres of Charborough estate that makes Drax and his family the largest individual landowners in Dorset. The mainly 17th-century mansion with its 120ft folly tower is the model for Welland House in the Thomas Hardy novel *Two on a Tower.*Richard Drax said of the Black Lives Matter protests.. "The desecration of the

Cenotaph by rioters two weeks ago, on the actual D-Day anniversary, was beyond ironic." As a reminder of the links between Dorset and Barbados a road that bisects the Charborough estate is called Sugar Hill. "The Drax family are one of the few who were pioneers in the early stages of the British slave economy back in the 17th century and, generations later, still owned plantations and enslaved people at the end of British slavery in the 1830s." - David Olusoga

CHAPTER ELEVEN

GYPSIES AND THE HOLOCAUST

IMAGES OF THE HOLOCAUST

No tomes of history can truly tell of these times
when the graceful hand of God was forsaken
for the wickedness of mankind
no writer, poet or critic with the pen

can truly state or record the tragedy or fate
or justify these actions of men too late

The courts of justice where Eichman declared with praise
the half million Gypsies slaughtered in the hostile craze
left rotting in their common graves
no music symphony can err compose
the tragedy of man kinds woes

Beware of the future yet to be
as another stone is set and another law enforced in history
we cannot accept the past with any real understandings
no photographic images or works of art
could ere depict
the horrors of that place so rich

As the tragedy of a mans worst crimes
fade into oblivion in the ranks of time
lest we forget the cries and tears
the Holocaust will disappear
forgotten for ever through the fading years

Ray Wills

SONGS FROM THE ASHES

We were herded like cattle
all branded together with the Z on our flesh
separated from our families
with no time for regrets

Husbands and wives
daughter and sons
some bodys darlings
then the horrors begun

Sisters and brothers all torn apart
no time for goodbyes or kisses goodnight in the dark
separated in wagons then we travelled by night
to such secret places kept by the Reich
I heared the cries of the frightened children in plight

All dressed in plain striped clothes all faded the same
now were just numbers and no ones to blame
Gypsy Roma all are no persons now
all no people of no name

The history books tell it
they tell it so well
the gas chambers of horrors
the camps and the smells

They cut off our hair and our dignity lost
then they gassed us there daily
neath the sign of the cross

Ray Wills

DEJA VU

He heard the stamping of their heavy feet
the lines were made with bodies starved of bread
the women wailing and the curse of men
millions were herded up and marched into concentration camps
Jews, non conformists, religious zealots.

Also amongst them were those called vagrants known as Roma
Gypsies
those who had over centuries fled numerous countries at the risk
of death or slavery
the air was full of death and the gas from within
the government official demanded papers
all were now injected regularly to avoid the epidemics

He thought back to the days when his people freely roamed the
country lanes and were respected
then he remembered
it starting with the signs on the public houses no gypsy travellers
and the land reforms and enclosure acts

Then later came the land snatchers and the cries of
lock down your goods in your garages, guard your valuables for
the travellers are coming
he remembered the headlines the common lies reeated by the
masses
workless layabouts, tax dodgers, dirty filth leaving their rubbish
behind them
He turned around and saw his brother led away
heard the wailing and smelt the gas in the air

he recalled the trespass laws imposed to stop all travellers from
staying overnight on common lands of what little remained

Was this a dream DEJA VU
he felt the heavy hand on his shoulder
and was led away.

Ray Wills

The Turn of the Wheel

Who set it in motion
who turned the tide
who caused the heartache
who told the lies
who heard their screams
who set the scene
who created the horror
who first had the dream

Who sanctioned the killings
who turned on the gas
who shut their ears
who made their last
who made it happen
who made the plans
who promised heaven
just a man

Herded like cattle
in trucks without hope
a people forgotten
a race time forgot
in the night of the killings
there was no shame or regrets
for a people of nomads
the story unfolds
thousands were slaughtered
of a race set apart
no reason or purpose

but to kill without shame
though the wheel it keeps turning
whilst no ones to blame

Ray Wills

Fascists in the 20th century turned also against the Roma. In Italy a circular went out in 1926 which ordered the expulsion of all foreign Roma in order to 'cleanse the country of Gypsy caravans which needless to recall, constitute a risk to safety and public health by virtue of the characteristic Gypsy lifestyle'. The order made clear that the aim was to 'strike at the heart of the Gypsy organism'. What followed in fascist Italy for the Roma was discrimination and persecution. Many were detained in special camps; others were sent to Germany or Austria and later exterminated."Like the Jews, Gypsies were singled out by the Nazis for racial persecution and annihilation. They were `non persons,' of `foreign blood,' `labour-shy,' and as such were termed asocials.

To a degree, they shared the fate of the Jews in their ghettos, in the extermination camps, before firing squads, as medical guinea pigs, and being injected with lethal substances. Ironically, the German writer Johann Christ of Wagenseil claimed in 1697 that Gypsies stemmed from German Jews.

In 1930s Nazi Germany, there was even a "comic" song about Gypsies as slaves, called "Come Gypsy; Show Me How You Can Work!". The song was adopted by the German press and quoted in headlines and articles to mock and denigrate German Roma, linking them to crime, brutality and squalor. Many European Roma were subsequently wiped out in the gas chambers and slave labour camps of the Third Reich – this holocaust is known in the Romany language as the Poraimos– or 'devouring'. It is the clear link between the denigration in the press of the Sinti and Roma in 1930's Germany and the discrimination and then subsequent enslavement and murder of between a half a million and a million of them by the Nazi regime less than a decade later.After the Nazis came to power in 1933, police in Germany began more rigorous enforcement of pre-Nazi legislation against Roma. The Nazis identified Roma as having "alien blood" (artfremdes Blut) and, therefore, as being racially "undesirable." The Law for the Protection of German Blood and German Honor, one of two Nurembergh Race Laws adopted by the Nazis in September 1935, was expanded in November to include the Romani population. The persecution of the Roma had started at the very beginning of the

Third Reich. Roma Gypsies were arrested and interned at concentration camps as well as sterilized under the July 1933 law for the Prevention of Hereditarily Diseased Offspring.

At the start they were not specifically named as a group that threatened the Aryan, German people. This was because, under Nazi racial ideology, Roma were Aryans.

The Nazi racial researchers came up with a reason to persecute most of the Roma adhering to the writings of Professor Hans F. K. Günther where he wrote: The Gypsies have indeed retained some elements from their Nordic home, but they are descended from the lowest classes of the population in that region. In the course of their migrations, they have absorbed the blood of the surrounding peoples, and have thus become an Oriental, western-Asiatic racial mixture, with an addition of Indian, mid-Asiatic, and European strains. Their nomadic mode of living is a result of this mixture. The Gypsies will generally affect Europe as aliens. The Nazis needed to determine who was "pure" Roma and who was "mixed."Thus, in 1936, the Nazis established the Racial Hygiene and Population Biology Research Unit, with Dr. Robert Ritter at its head, to study the Roma "problem" and to make recommendations for Nazi policy. As with the Jews, the Nazis had to ascertain who amongst them were to be considered as a "Gypsy." Dr. Robert Ritter, a physician at the University of Tuebingen, became the central figure in the study of Roma. His speciality was criminal biology; that is, the idea that criminal behaviour is genetically determined. In 1936, Ritter became the director of the Center for Research on Racial Hygiene and Demographic Biology in the Ministry of Health and began a racial study of Roma. Ritter undertook to locate and classify by racial type Roma living in Germany, often collaborating with the police. He estimated that the Roma and Sinti population in Germany at the time was around 30,000. He performed medical and anthropometric examinations in an attempt to classify Roma. Dr. Ritter decided that someone could be considered a Gypsy only if they had "one or two Gypsies among his grandparents."Dr. Robert Ritter, wrote in 1940: "Gypsies [are] a people of entirely primitive ethnological origins, whose mental backwardness makes them incapable of real social adaptation. The

Gypsy question can only be solved when. the good-for-nothing Gypsy individuals. [are] in large labour camps and kept working there, and when further breeding of this population. is stopped once and for all." or if "two or more of his grandparents are part-Gypsies." Kenrick and Puxon blame Dr. Ritter for the additional 18,000 German Roma who were killed because of this more inclusive designation, rather than if the same rules had been followed as were applied to Jews, who needed three or four Jewish grandparents to be considered Jews.

From their research they established that 90% of Roma were of mixed blood, and thus dangerous. Many wanted all Roma killed, with no exceptions. That they were a Gypsy menace. By the end of the war, an estimated 250,000 to 500,000 Roma were murdered in the Porajmos approximately three-fourths of the German Roma and half of the Austrian Roma were killed.All over Germany, both local citizens and local police detachments began forcing Roma into municipal camps. Later, these camps evolved into forced-labour camps for Roma. Marzahn and the Gypsy camps (Zigeunerlager) set up in other cities between 1935 and 1938 were a preliminary stage on the road to genocide. The men from Marzahn, for example, were sent to Sachsenhausen in 1938 and their families were deported to Auschwitz in 1943.Prior to the Holocaust, Roma in Nazi Germany became subject to the Nuremberg Race Laws (1935) and the Law for the Prevention of Hereditarily Diseased Progeny (1933). Roma were also criminalised under the Law against Dangerous Habitual Criminals (1933). These acts led to the forced sterilisation of Roma and their incarceration in prison or concentration camps. Roma were forcibly relocated to tightly guarded encampments where their freedom of movement was restricted. Treatment by authorities and institutional racism.The Nazi regime defined the Roma (including the Sinti) as 'racially inferior' with an 'asocial behaviour' which was deemed hereditary. This, in fact, was a development of old and widespread prejudices in both Germany and Austria. The so-called Nürnberg race laws of 1935 deprived the Roma of their nationality and citizen's rights. It was demanded that they should be interned into labour camps and sterilised by force.

The relevance of Roma persecution in Nazi Germany has never subsided. Between 1936 and 1976, 60,000 Romani women in Sweden were sterilised. Persecution of Roma (Gypsies) in Pre-war Germany and throughout Europe preceded the Nazi takeover of power in 1933. For example, in 1899, the police in the German state of Bavaria, formed the Central Office for Gypsy Affairs (Zigeunerzentrale) to coordinate police action against Roma in the city of Munich. This office compiled a central registry of Roma that grew to include data on Roma and Sinti from other German states. A main concern for the Nazis was the systematic identification of all Romani people, whom they labelled "Gypsies." A definition of "Gypsy," therefore, was essential in order to undertake systematic persecution of the Romani population. To do this, the Nazis turned to "racial hygiene" (Rassenhygiene), also known as eugenics. Using this pseudo-science, they sought to determine who was Romani based on physical characteristics. Dr Ritters team of researchers interviewed Roma to determine and record their genealogy, often under the threat of arrest and incarceration in concentration camps unless they identified their relatives and their last known residence.

At the conclusion of his study, Dr Ritter declared that although Roma had originated in India and were therefore once Aryan, they had been corrupted by mingling with lesser peoples during their long migration to Europe. Ritter estimated that some 90 percent of all Roma in Germany were of mixed blood and were consequently carriers of "degenerate" blood and criminal characteristics. Because they allegedly constituted a danger, Ritter recommended they be forcibly sterilized. The remaining pure-blooded Roma, Ritter argued, should be studied further. In practice, little distinction was made between Ritter's so-called pure-blooded and mixed-blooded Roma. They all became subject to the Nazi policy of persecution and, later, mass murder. A more contemporary Nazi theorist believed that `the Gypsy cannot, by reason of his inner and outer makeup (Konstruktion), be a useful member of the human community.'The Nuremberg Laws of 1935 aimed at the Jews were soon amended to include the Gypsies. In 1937, they were classified as asocials, second-class citizens, subject to concentration camp imprisonment. As early as 1936, some had been sent to camps. Nazi spokesman George Nawrocki had this to say in 1937: "It was in keeping with the inner weakness and mendacity of the Weimar Republic that it showed no instinct for tackling the Gypsy question. We, on the other hand, see the Gypsy question as above all a racial problem, which must be solved and which is being solved."Shortly before the opening of the 1936 Olympic games in Berlin, the police ordered the arrest and forcible relocation of all Roma in Greater Berlin to Marzhan, an open field located near a cemetery and sewage dump in eastern Berlin. Police surrounded all Romani encampments and transported the inhabitants and their wagons to Marzahn, while others were arrested in their apartments. Uniformed police guarded the camp, restricting free movement into and out of the camp, while the criminal police (Kripo) supervised the camp itself. Many of the Roma incarcerated there continued going to work every day, but were required to return each night. Later, they were compelled to perform forced labor in armaments plants.

Roma became subject to the Nuremberg Race Laws shortly after the laws were passed in 1935. They were also subject to the Law for the Prevention of Hereditarily Diseased Progeny and the Law against Dangerous Habitual Criminals. Many Roma who came to the attention of the state were required to be sterilized.

In 1936, the Nazis centralized all police power in Germany under Henrich Himmler, SS chief and chief of the German police. Consequently, police policy toward Roma *View This Term in the Glossary* was also centralized. Himmler relocated the Central Office for Gypsy Affairs from Munich to Berlin. In Berlin, he established the Reich Central Office for the Suppression of the Gypsy Nuisance as part of the criminal police (Kripo). This agency took over and extended bureaucratic measures to systematically persecute Roma.An earlier plan of Nazi racists to keep some of the 'racially pure' Roma in a sort of anthropological museum was forgotten, while some Roma, not least children, were singled out for Josef Mengele's cruel medical experiments. A policy of forced sterilisation was implemented, often without anaesthesia.

Adolf Eichmann on regarding the transport of Gypsies in a telegram from Vienna to the Gestapo stated: Regarding transport of Gypsies be informed that on Friday, October 20, 1939, the first transport of Jews will depart Vienna. To this transport 3-4 cars of Gypsies are to be attached. Subsequent trains will depart from Vienna, Mahrisch-Ostrau and Katowice [Poland]. The simplest method is to attach some carloads of Gypsies to each transport. Because these transports must follow schedule, a smooth execution of this matter is expected. Concerning a start in the Altreich [Germany proper] be informed that this will be coming in 3-4 weeks. Eichmann. Himmler initially wished to exempt two tribes of Gypsies and `only' sterilize them, but by 1942 he had signed the decree for all Gypsies to be shipped to Auschwitz. There they were subjected to all that Auschwitz meant, including the medical experiments, before they were exterminated.The systematic murder of Roma started in the summer 1941 when German troops attacked the Soviet Union. They were seen as spies (like many Jews) for the 'Jewish Bolshevism' and were shot by the German army and the SS in mass executions. Indeed, in all areas occupied by the Nazis there were executions of Roma people. Figures remain uncertain, but it is estimated that far more than hundred thousand were executed in those situations, including in the Balkans where the killings were supported by local fascists. The Ustascha militia in Croatia ran camps but also organised deportations and carried out mass executions.

The fascist 'Iron Guard' regime in Romania started deportations in 1942. Like many Jews, about 30.00 Roma were brought across the river Dniester where they suffered hunger, disease and death. Only about half of them managed to survive the two years of extreme hardship before the policy changed.In France about 6,000 Roma were interned during the war, the majority of them in the occupied zone. Unlike other victims, the Roma were not systematically released upon the German retreat. The new French authorities saw internment as a means of forcing them to settle. The National Socialists designated Gypsies, along with Jews, for annihilation. They rounded up the Gypsies for "protective custody," and shipped them off to concentration camps. Gypsy persons were forcibly sterilized, the subjects of medical experiments, injected with typhus, worked to death, starved to death, froze to death, and gassed in various numbers.

The total dead at the hands of the Nazis is estimated to be 275,000.After 1939, Gypsies from Germany and from the German-occupied territories were shipped by the thousands first to Jewish ghettos in Poland at Warsaw, Lublin, Kielce, Rabka, Zary, Siedlce and others.Many were killed by the Einsatzgruppen charged with speedy extermination by shooting. For the sake of efficiency Gypsies were also shot naked, facing their pre-dug graves. According to the Nazi experts, shooting Jews was easier, they stood still, 'while the Gypsies cry out, howl, and move constantly, even when they are already standing on the shooting ground. Some of them even jumped into the ditch before the volley and pretended to be dead.' The first to go were the German Gypsies; 30,000 were deported East in three waves in 1939, 1941 and 1943. Gypsies married to Germans were exempted but were sterilized, as were their children after the age of twelve. Gypsies perished in Dachau, Mauthausen, Ravensbruck and other camps. Whilst at Sachsenhausen they were subjected to special experiments that were to prove scientifically that their blood was different from that of the Germans. The doctors in charge of this.In the Baltic States a large number of the Roma inhabitants were killed by the German invasion forces and their local supporters within the police. Only 5-10 per cent of the Roma in Estonia survived. In Latvia about half of the Roma were shot while it is estimated that a vast majority of those in Lithuania were also killed. All countries in Europe were affected by the racist ideas of the time. In the neutral Sweden the authorities had encouraged a sterilisation program already in the twenties which primarily targeted the Roma (and which continued up to the seventies). Also in Norway pressure was exerted on Roma to sterilise.In December 1942, the Nazi regime decided that all Roma in the 'German Reich' should be deported to Auschwitz. There they had to wear a dark triangle and a Z was tattooed to their arm. Of all camp inmates they had the highest death rate: 19,300 lost their lives there. Of them 5,600 were gassed and 13,700 died from hunger, disease or following medical experiments.

The deportations and executions of the Gypsies came under Himmler's authority. On December 16th He issued an order to send all Gypsies to the concentration camps, with a few exceptions. The deported Gypsies were sent to Auschwitz-Birkenau, where a special Gypsy camp was erected. Over 20,000 Gypsies from Germany and some other parts of Europe were sent to this camp, According to the The Institut Fuer Zeitgeschicthe, in Munich, at least 4000 Gypsies were murdered by gas there.

Wiernik described the arrival of the largest Gypsy group brought to Treblinka, in the spring of 1943: "One day, while I was working near the gate, I noticed the Germans and Ukrainians making special preparations…meanwhile the gate opened, and about 1,000 Gypsies were brought in (this was the third transport of Gypsies). About 200 of them were men, and the rest women and children…all the Gypsies were taken to the gas chambers and then burned".

This passive denial of the grim facts could not have been surprising to the Roma themselves, as for generations they had been treated as a people without history. The violations they had suffered were quickly forgotten, if even recognised. Sadly, this same pattern is repeated even today. The Roma were seen as unreliable, dangerous, criminal, and undesirable. They were the outsiders who could easily be used as scapegoats when things went wrong and the locals did not want to take responsibility.In Wallachia and Moldavia (today's Romania) the Roma lived in slavery and bondage for centuries up to 1855 when the last Roma slaves were finally emancipated.It is still not known how many Roma in total fell victim to the Nazi persecution. Not all Roma were registered as Roma and the records are incomplete. The fact that there was no reliable statistics about the number of Roma in these areas before the mass killings makes it even more difficult to estimate the actual number of casualties. The Council of Europe fact sheets state that it is highly probable that the number was at least 250,000. Other credible studies indicate that more than 500,000 Roma lost their lives, perhaps many more. Gypsies from the General Government [Poland] who were not sent to Auschwitz and to the operation Reinhard camps were shot on spot by the local police or gendarmes.

In the eastern region of the Cracow district, in the counties of Sanok, Jaslo, and Rzeszow, close to 1,000 Gypsies were shot."

The Roma ("Gypsies") of Europe were registered, sterilized, ghetto sized, and then deported to concentration and death camps by the Nazis before and during World War II. Approximately 250,000 to 500,000 Roma people were murdered during the Holocaust—an event they call the Porajmos (the "Devouring.")In recent times the persecution of Gypsies persists especially in Central and Eastern Europe where Roma make up ten percent of the population (Bulgaria, Slovakia, Romania). They were discriminated against under communism, and now their plight has dramatically worsened since. Their endemic problems continue and now include low life expectancy, high illiteracy, dire poverty, poor housing and disproportionate unemployment. In recent times their unprecedented persecution has persisted by new state nationalism and easing of censorship. Gypsies were often blamed for many atrocities committed by others; including looting of gold teeth from a hundred dead Jews abandoned on a Rumanian road. Gypsy women were forced to become guinea pigs in the hands of Nazi physicians.

Among others they were sterilized as `unworthy of human reproduction' (fortpflanzungsunwuerdig), only to be ultimately annihilated as not worthy of living. At that, the Gypsies were the luckier ones; in Bulgaria, Greece, Denmark and Finland they were spared.

THE NIGHT OF THE GYPSIES

On August 2/3 1944 the German SS rounded up the Gypsies luring them out of the barrack with the promise of water and bread. Once the Gypsies realised they fought back with their bare hands but they were no match for the clubs and guns of the SS and were put into vehicles and driven to the gas chambers. As most Gypsies at that time were elitterit many were not registered at the camps and if they were registered a plain Z was put on their forms. The vast majority were either killed in transportation or before or where they were taken or captured, consequently there were no records of their deaths. According to Ian Hiscock." The family camps were not created out of any humanitarian motive, but because Roma became completely unmanageable when being seperated from family members. It was simply more expedient and caused the guards less problems, to leave families together for processing yet referred to only Roma people and not to the Jews." For a while there was a Gypsy Family Camp in Auschwitz, but on August 6,1944, it was liquidated. Some men and women were shipped to German factories as slave labour; the rest, about 3,000 women, children and old people, were gassed. No precise statistics exist about the extermination of European Gypsies. Some estimates place the number between 500,000 and 600,000, most of them gassed in Auschwitz. Others indicated a more conservative 200,000 Gypsy victims of the Holocaust."Roma were also arrested as "asocials" or "habitual criminals" and sent to concentration camps. Nearly every concentration camp in Germany had Romani prisoners. In the camps, all prisoners wore Markings of various shapes and colours, which identified them by category of prisoner. Roma typically wore black triangular patches, the symbol for "asocials."Everyone of us are all aware of the fact that Six million Jews were killed in the Nazi Holocaust. There were an estimated 5.5 million "enemies of the German State" who were murdered under equally inhumane circumstances-- criminals and a-socials, the insane, homosexuals, Jehovah's Witnesses, political criminals such as communists and socialists, and of course the Gypsies.

Only a few thousand Roma in Germany survived the Holocaust and the concentration camps. They faced enormous difficulties when trying to build up their lives again, having lost so many of their family members and relatives, and having had their properties destroyed or confiscated. Many of them had their health ruined. When some of them tried to obtain compensation, their claims were rejected for years. For these survivors no justice came with the post-Hitler era. Significantly, the mass killing of the Roma people was not an issue at the Nürnberg trial. The genocide of the Roma – *Samudaripe or Porrajmos*– was hardly recognised in the public discourse. A Hungarian Roma survivor stated "They cut off our hair and everything to be hairless. It was done by women, then a doctor examined us thoroughly.. They examined you know everything. He was the one who gave the injection to me and to all the others to everybody. It hurt badly You know he gave me an injection down there. Everything went black I fell off the examining table. They kicked me away it was time for the next. They gave me an injection like that one and after that I did not have that monthly thing." Roma are just like the Jews once were are now the main scapegoat for society's ills. They are frequently stigmatized by all areas of the media. Only a few countries have enforced laws to protect their human rights. Some activists fear a potential genocide if conditions worse.

Today's rhetoric against the Roma is very similar to the one used by Nazis and fascists before the mass killings started in the thirties and forties. Once more, it is argued that the Roma is a threat to safety and public health. No distinction is made between a few criminals and the overwhelming majority of the Roma population. This is shameful and dangerous.

CHAPTER TWELVE

GYPSY FUTURES AND HERITAGE

Freedom chants

When morning broke in the land of the free
the hands of the clock chimed for liberty
the anarchic fools studied the law
then resolved their complex science in a rhyme
the padre quoted the bibles prayers
whilst foolish virgins climbed the stairs

The jackals barked at the break of the day
whilst all Gods children looked for a place to play
the lost soldiers wandered o'er barren lands
where oil rich sultans set their plans
the square and compass set the rules
for wayward girls and forgetful fools

The band did play its final march
as politician's played their games in the dark
the wars were over they said twas true
as they stored more weapons in the minds of fools
the quarrelsome doctors branded anew
their potent drugs to solve the blues

Whilst a lonesome crooner sang his song
the pretty dancing girls paraded with nothing on
the curtain fell and the act was through

as mankind threw out the golden rule
along with babies yet to die
the clown he smiled and winked an eye
All across the world of spin
the actors bowed and the set begins
the speech that the prophet read out loud
was drowned in tears and widows cries

Ray Wills

Denmark-Norway was the first European country to ban the slave trade. This happened with a decree issued by Kin Christian VII of Denmark in 1792, to become fully effective by 1803.Whilst Napoleon Bonaparte re established slavery in Guadeloupe and Martinique in 1804, at the request of planters of the Caribbean colonies.William Wilberforce led Britain's slavery reform when Parliament passed the Slave Trade Act in 1807. Though British slaves were not finally emancipated by Act of the British Parliament until 1834. Then large amounts of monies in compensation were paid by the British government to slave industry stake-holders including amongst them the Bishop of Exeter and three business colleagues for their loss of 665 slaves. In 1839 Britain finally decided to stop transporting slaves. Whilst in Romania there were up to a quarter of a million Tzigani Gypsy slaves. Slavery as an institution was not banned until 1848. At this time Iceland was a part of Denmark-Norway slave trading had been abolished in Iceland in 1117 and had never been re established. In Romania, 200,000 Gypsy persons were still enslaved in the first half of the nineteenth century. They worked as grooms, coachmen, cooks, barbers, tailors, farriers, comb makers, and domestic servants. Their masters could kill them with impunity.One reformer described the treatment of these slaves in Iasi: "human beings wearing chains on their arms and legs, others with iron clamps round their foreheads. Cruel floggings and other punishments, such as starvation, being hung over smoking fires, being thrown naked into a frozen river. children torn from the breasts of those who brought them into the world, and sold like cattle."

The outbreak of war in Europe in 1939 and subsequent conscription, meant that Gypsies were a useful source of labour for the war effort. Gypsies were also victims of the Nazi regime.

After the 1939-1945 war the Sinti and Roma Gypsies were required to register with the local German police and the criminal identification service. By 1948 the central criminal department of Baden Wurtenburgh issued guidelines to the police for the fight against the Gypsy menace. New laws were implemented based on the former 1926 Law for the fight against Gypsies and idlers.

In 1956 the German Federal Court stated that the Roma and Snti deportation to the concentration camps had not been a persecution out of racial reasons, but a pre emptive criminal measure. Compensation and support for reintegration was denied to them and photos and fingerprints were to be kept on file. The Soviet Union decreed that the last wandering Gypsies there should be gradually settled in a place of their own choice. Similar countries of East Europe, where the vast majority of Gypsies were grateful to find safety there.

In 1984,Simon Wiesenthal wrote that the Gypses had been murdered in a proportion similar as the Jews, about 80 percent of them in all the countries which were occupied by the Nazis.In many countries around the world such as at Czechoslovakia Gypsies were forced into settlements, their horses were slaughtered and their wagons burned. Many were not permitted to travel and all their valuables and money was taken. All their independent groups and newspapers were closed down. Were as in Yogoslavia it was a different story, the media TV and radio stations gave broadcasts in the Romani language. Many Gypsies there began to participate in regional politics and hundreds of them gained work as doctors, lawyers and engineers. In the UK in 1959 the new Highways Act made it illegal for Gypsies to camp along sides the road. Many Gypsies found difficulty in finding employment or to have their children attend schools. It was then that local councils began moving the Gypsies from the compounds into council housing. In 1965 following a study Gypsies were housed and found work

THE NEW FOREST ENCAMPMENTS

England

In 1926 the Forest commission found an answer to the problem of Gypsies living in the New Forest. Its solution was to confine them to compounds where like the native American Indians on reservations they could be corralled within the forest in which they had once roamed free.. Forbidden from building any permanent structures, these were issued with six months licences which could be revoked instantly should their behaviour upset the commission. Their compounds were in effect no more than concentration camps. Movements between these compounds were not restricted but Gypsies were forbidden to camp outside of them. There were no toilets and limited waiter supply, living in the compounds interfered with the Gypsies normal way of life because they had preferred to live in small family units rather than a community/ This often led to trouble, disagreements and many arguments between families.

The system also interfered restricted the gypsy families earning potential because they were no longer able to travel and earn an honest living as they had previously. This system in many aspects was not unlike the native American or the German concentration area. Rather than rather than live in these compounds sone families actually moved out of the new forest altogether. By the 1930s, the population of the 7 compounds had reached nearly one thousand swollen by the effects of the depression.

By 1960 The Caravan Sites Act of 1960 made it difficult for Gypsies and Travellers to buy and winter on small plots of land, unless they had a licence that could only be gained through planning permission. Even those staying on the private land of farmers they were working for, could no longer do so. The effect of this was to push even more Gypsies and Travellers on to the roadside. In 1965 a national survey d 'Gypsies and Other Travellers findings showed that 60% of the families had travelled in the previous year, mainly as a result of harassment from police and council officials. 1968 Caravan Sites Act provisions: Many Gypsies and Traveller have traditionally worked along side their residing place testament of this.

Romania, in the early 1970s, tried to obliterate Gypsy culture and force the Gypsies into squalid ghettos. Their valuables were confiscated, including their favorite form of savings—huge old gold coins. Bulgaria forbade Gypsies to travel and closed their associations and newspapers

In 1989, The Race Relations Act saw that Romani Gypsies were at last confirmed as an ethnic group. However, true Romani connections may have to be established in order to prove a case of discrimination. This legislation means that it is now a criminal offence to discriminate against those of Gypsy origin on account of their race.After the industrial revolution and the mechanisation of farming the lifestyles of Gypsies had changed dramatically. They were no longer required for hop or strawberry picking and other traditional trades. Once again Gypsies had to adapt and found finding work difficult whilst the motorisation of families changed travel patterns. The changes in society were also reflected in the Roma population. Many Gypsies moved from rural areas to cities and towns.

The new National Curriculum launched by the government in September 2014 was intended to focus on the celebration of British history. Unfortunately In practice, this has meant that diverse histories such as Roma history have been completely ignored. Roma communities continue to be among the most monitored and restricted communities in Europe. Reports of targeted and disproportionate action against Roma remain widespread throughout Europe. Since the beginning of government-led lockdowns in Europe, uniformed guarding and freedom of movement restrictions imposed on Roma encampments and villages in Bulgaria, Italy and Slovakia have mirrored that of Nazi Germany. Marginalisation and disproportionate action against Roma has continued and in many European countries, it is entrenched and systematically imposed. In Europe today, Roma face inferior, and in many cases segregated, housing and education.A report published by the European Parliament in April 2020 stated that in Slovakia: At the primary school level, Roma children encounter school segregation and discriminatory practices, extensive and unjustified enrolment in ethnically segregated special schools and classes. Roma poverty and low employment levels A 2014 joint report by the Fundamental Rights Agency,In the middle of the 19th century there were half a million slaves on Romanian territory 70 per cent of the population. Unfortunately, until now, Roma slavery has not been yet included in most history school books, and there are still very few Romanians who are aware of this historical reality.

Roma people represent the second most widely-spread ethnic minority and the most vulnerable ethnic group in Romania. Even though the process of Roma integration began more than 15 years ago, the results leave much to be desired. Tackling discrimination of Roma people is still more of an empty promise than a reality. Now days the Gypsy, Roma and Traveller communities continue to experience open discrimination and prejudice, both in the UK and throughout Europe.

The discrimination and adverse life chances faced by Gypsy, Roma and Traveller populations in the UK and Europe have continued to remain a problem for decades. Reports from the Commission for racial equality (in 2006), the Equality and Human Rights Commission(in 2010) and the European Commission (in 2018) have rigorously documented the inequalities and discrimination faced by these communities. The most recent of these confirmed that countries with larger Roma populations experienced an increase in anti-Roma hate speech, segregated and poor accommodation, even as hundreds of thousands of Roma endured a lack of access to basic services including clean water and sanitation.With the steady arrival of Roma from central and eastern Europe to the UK, there's a real risk of replicating the hostile anti-Roma environment seen in much of central and eastern Europe, which forces such communities to flee and polarises neighbourhoods.

The UK government's record on Roma issues has been one of inaction and neglect. Plans, such as the coalition 2012 strategy inequalities have been widely divided for having limited scope, little ambition and weak recommendations. The most recent inquiry failed to consider the shortage of pitches and site accommodation across the UK, which many groups representing Roma, Gypsy and Traveller communities would consider to be one of the most pressing concerns.

Yet the report represents a significant intervention against government inaction and hostile policy making. Few politicians – with notable exceptions such as Kate Green and Baronness Whitaker – speak out against the inequalities faced by Gypsy, Roma and Traveller communities. Indeed, during the inquiry, Conservative MP Jackie Doyle-Price said: "Let's be honest: we are all Members of Parliament and we all know there are no votes in championing this group of people".

Gypsy, Roma and Traveller communities, on average, continue to die far younger than members of other communities and have poorer health than members of other communities. They also experience the death of a child far frequently than other communities. The needs and position of Gypsy, Roma and Traveller communities are so stark that considered steps must be taken.

So this should be an opportunity for the government and other public bodies to take more forceful and co-ordinated action. One way forward is for the government to use the Ravce Disparity Audit to address inequalities. Vocal leadership is also required from within government at all levels.

For far too long, Gypsy, Roma and Traveller communities have been used as a political football, with few people in positions of power speaking up for their needs.

Successive governments have tried doing nothing, pilot projects have been attempted and main streaming the needs of Gypsy, Roma and Traveller communities has been the recent approach. But all have failed over the long term or led to very little improvement. Government needs to lead and to foster leadership in others. There has been no coordinated plans and actions to resolve the issues. As in most areas, resources will also be an issue, but a desire and an ability to affect change is critical. In doing so, the UK will address some of the long standing issues for Gypsy, Roma and Traveller people and make communities more equal and less hostile places.

Fake news, disinformation, conspiracy theories all abound.

Gypsies have always excited hatred in the press. For hundreds of years they have played a small but lively part in the European imagination, and these days, when so much of public discourse is deadened by euphemism, Gypsies are perhaps the last group up for grabs. (Is the beggar named as Maria Nistor going to complain when a reporter - the Sun again-claims that she has named her baby "Lucifer"?) These familiar strangers are regarded monolithically; their given name is a synonym for thieves and cheats. As beggars and as Gypsies they are now also emblematic of all asylum seekers: beggars and presumed cheats at the gate of the west. But it is readers who are being "gypped". For in page after page of pious press coverage, myth has displaced history and opinion has displaced facts either about their circumstances or about immigration policy.Gypsies are profoundly mistrustful of outside influences: understandable, when you consider the draconian drives, at least in eastern and central Europe, to assimilate them.

Since the 18th century such measures have included the removal of Gypsy children into Christian institutions and homes (a practice continued in Switzerland until 1973), and, under the communists, the compulsory changing of Gypsy names. All in all, in any interaction with non-Gypsies, at home or abroad, they live in tense anticipation of ill-will, bad faith, rejection and harm. If children are toughened by what they see, their parents may feel that this is appropriate training for an expected lifetime of hate directed at them.

The lives of Gypsies, since they left India at the beginning of the last millennium, has consisted of deportation and nomadism, homelessness and statelessness, interwoven with episodes of forced assimilation as well as incarceration and massacre. In Romania, where most of these recent arrivals come from, Gypsies were slaves for 400 years, until 1864 when slavery was abolished in Romania.

Under the Nazis, at least half a million were murdered. Gypsies were the only group apart from the Jews slated for annihilation on racial grounds. Gypsies have only recently begun to commemorate their Holocaust dead, but they remain without a homeland. These periods of extreme persecution are reasonably regarded by them as forming part of the great continuum of persecution. It would not be far-fetched to wonder whether, in the case of the Gypsies, "nomad" is perhaps nothing more than a travel agent's kind of term for "deportee".

In my home county of Dorset many of our wealthy aristocratic respectable gentlemen and their families were involved in the colonialism and the slave trade. Along with its trade to such countries as Newfoundland and Africa in particular. Many Dorset towns and ports were involved in the slave trade to and from the plantations of the West Indies. With many prominent local Dorset families at the forefront. By the end of the 17th century many of our local ports were sending expeditions to Africa to buy or barter for slaves. With black slaves providing labour for the plantations of the West Indies and Americas. Our merchants gained a lucrative trade exporting products to Africa and the American continent. Carrying slaves from Africa to the colonies then returning with plantation produce such as sugar and tobacco. Most of these African slaves spent their lives labouring on the plantation all provided great wealth for our merchants. However some were brought here by the plantation owners, captains of slave ships and our local merchants involved in the slave trade. Such slaves were often sold on here to others to local prosperous families. Such families included those of Richard Hellett a Barbados plantation estate owner brought with him a retinue of black servant slaves when he returned home to Lyme Regis in 1699 and his wife Meliora Hallett likewise brought one or two black servants with her. As recorded in local censuses of 1695-1703. Others heavily involved in the local slave trade included Robert Burridge, along with Walter Tucker. The Burridges and the Drax families. Their families dominance of the African trade was supported by money, expertise and the merchandise supplied not only by the inhabitants of Lyme Regis but also by all the many other ports of the Dorset area. The Burridge family never became plantation owners themselves, but they were at times slave owners. Part of their payment of commission for a venture was sometimes taken in the slave trade. These provided the colonies of the West Indies and America with necessary items and imported sugar and tobacco.

In the 18th century the Burridges were taking a leading role in sending slave ships to new Guinea. They used all local ports and were the main traders from the port of Lyme Regis for decades from around 1713. Their successful enterprises during this time involved them working alongside local traders and merchants. The families book contain numerous referenced to slaves. Their slave ship *Martha* gives an entry of 200 slaves with some 160 of them bound for Jamaica in March 1710. In June of that year their ship *Martha* arrived in Bristol with plantation produce of sugar, indigo and lime juice. Shortly after the *Martha* was lost at sea to French privateers. The family commenced their slave trade shortly after with a new slave ship in 1712 called *Mary and Elizabeth.* Their other ship *John Frigate* was itself a small vessel of just 65 tons and went on a mammoth 3 years voyage to the West Indies and the Americas before returning to Barbados with 91 slaves before returning to Lyme Regis.It was no doubt that whilst on these numerous ventures they probably obtained their slaves from African kings or from middlemen or women, either by purchase bartering in exchange for a variety of goods, the most common being cloth. Other items much in demand as slave goods was copper, iron bas, gunpowder, tallow, whisky, and tobacco. The notorious packing of slaves below deck was horrific at times causing much misery and discomfort. It is known that the mortality rate on board The Burridge slave ships was very high. For instance on the journey to Gambia in 1712 of the 200 slaves onboard the *Mary Elizabeth* on landing in Virginia the ships master reported that there were113 still alive. Another local slave trader was John Pitts who was a merchant of Lyme Regis and involved with the Burridges.

British Royalty who supported the slave trade

Elizabeth 1
The Tudor queen gave a large royal ship to the slave trader John Hawkins in 1564 in exchange for a share in the profits of his voyage. During his trip he captured many African people and seized 600 more from Portuguese ships.

James I
The first Stuart king granted royal-connected merchants a monopoly on trade with Africa. They formed the Guinea Company, which provided enslaved people for English-owned tobacco plantations in Virginia, America.

Charles I (1625-1649)
The king granted a monopoly licence to the reconstituted Guinea Company in 1632 to transport enslaved people. English colonies were established where the economies were based on the exploitation of enslaved people's labour, beginning with Barbados, in 1636.

King Charles II
He gave the Company of Royal Adventurers of England a royal charter. He was the first king after the monarchy was restored, following England's brief period as a republic, in effect made the slave trade a state-sponsored enterprise. He invested in a slave-trading business, the Company of Royal Adventurers of England Trading into Africa, and gave it a royal charter. When the company was dissolved in 1672, the king moved his patronage to the Royal African Company. This company would transport more enslaved people from Africa to the Americas than any other single organisation in the history of the transatlantic trade.

James II (1685-1688)
He was governor of the Royal African Company and was awarded 500 guineas for his "extraordinary services" in 1677. As king he was the company's largest shareholder until he sold the shares after

he was deposed in the "Glorious Revolution" of 1688. According to the most conservative estimate. James made £6,210 from his investment – equivalent to £1m today.

William III and Mary II (1689-1694)
The Dutch prince William of Orange, a protestant, supplanted James II, who was Catholic, in the "Glorious Revolution". In January 1689, He accepted a free transfer of £1000 in shares (equivalent to £163,000 today) in the Royal African Company from its deputy governor, the now notorious Edward Colston.

Queen Anne
She is remembered for the union of England and Scotland in 1707, which formed the United Kingdom of Great Britain. She also dramatically expanded the nation's slave-trading activities by securing from Spain in 1713 the Asiento de negros, a monopoly right to supply enslaved African people to Spain's colonies in South America. This contract was fulfilled by the South Sea Company.

George I
He was governor of the South Sea Company and held a substantial shareholding.

George II
He too was a governor and shareholder of the South Sea Company. The company which took 41,923 African captives on its ships between 1714 and 1740. More than 7,000 people died on the voyages.

George III (1760-1820)
He supported the continuation of the slave trade and slavery, and opposed the abolition movement behind the scenes.

George IV's
His lack of support for the growing movement to abolish slavery also helped to delay emancipation for years. His reign was marked by ruthless suppression of uprisings by enslaved people in the Caribbean. British authorities reacted with a massacre, on-the-spot

executions, and sentences of whipping. Ten enslaved people who rebelled were hanged then decapitated, and their heads were displayed on spikes.

William IV

He was king when slavery was abolished in 1833, but he had always opposed abolition. Before becoming king, he held the title Duke of Clarence and spent time in the Caribbean, where he befriended plantation owners. He devoted speeches in the Lords defending slavery, arguing that it was vital to prosperity, and that enslaved people were "comparatively in a state of humble happiness".

CHAPTER THIRTEEN

MODERN TIMES

Contemporary slavery, also known as modern slavery or neo-slavery, refers to institutional slavery. It still exists and continues to occur in present-day society. Despite all the international laws.

Estimates of the number of enslaved people in the world today range from around 38 million to 46 million. The International Labour Organisation recently estimates that over 40 million people are in some form of slavery today. Of these 24.9 million people are in forced labour, of whom 16 million people are exploited in the private sector such as domestic work, construction or agriculture; 4.8 million persons in forced sexual exploitation, and 4 million persons in forced labour imposed by state authorities.

Modern slavery', known as 'trafficking in persons', and human trafficking' have been used as umbrella terms for the act of recruiting, harbouring, transporting, providing or obtaining a person for compelled labour or commercial sex acts through the use of force, fraud, or coercion. There are a variety of different terms used for this practice which include those of "involuntary servitude", "slavery" or "practices similar to slavery", "debt bondage", and "forced labour".

According to American professor Kevin Bates modern slavery occurs "when a person is under the control of another person who applies violence and force to maintain that control, and the goal of that control is exploitation".

Recent research estimates that there were about 40.3 million slaves around the world in 2018. Kevin Bates warned that, because slavery is officially abolished everywhere, the practice is illegal, and thus more hidden from the public and authorities. This makes it impossible to obtain exact figures from primary sources. Modern slavery persists for many of the same reasons older variations did: it is an economically beneficial practice despite the ethical concerns. The problem has been able to escalate in recent years due to the *disposability* of slaves and the fact that the cost of slaves has dropped significantly.

Since slavery has been officially abolished, enslavement no longer revolves around legal ownership, but around illegal control. Two fundamental changes are the move away from the forward purchase of slave labour, and the existence of slaves as an employment category. Statistics suggest that the 'market' for exploitative labour is booming, the notion that humans are purposefully sold and bought from an existing pool is outdated. While such basic transactions do still occur, in contemporary cases people become trapped in slavery-like conditions in various ways.

Modern slavery is often seen as a by-product of poverty. In countries which lack education and the rule of law. In countries where there are poor societal structure this can create an environment that fosters the acceptance and propagation of slavery. Slavery is most prevalent in these impoverished countries particularly those which have vulnerable minority communities, though slavery also exists in developed countries. Tens of thousands of people toil in slave-like conditions in numerous labour intensive industries such as mining, farming, and factories, which produce goods for domestic consumption or export goods to more prosperous nations.In the older form of slavery, such as in colonial times those slavers who created the cotton and sugar plantations spent more on getting their slaves. They needed these slaves to be fit and healthy and to be able to man their vast plantation estates. It was more difficult for them to dispose of their slaves to be disposed of. For many it became obvious that the cost of keeping their slaves healthy was considered a far better investment then than going through the rigours of obtaining strong healthy and reliable workers at a fair price as reliable replacements. In modern times slavery people are easier to get at a lower price so replacing them when exploiters run into problems becomes easier. Slaves in our modern world are used in areas where they could easily be hidden from society and more attractive for unpleasant work and less for more pleasant work. Whilst obviously creating a profit for the present day exploiter. Modern slavery can be quite profitable, and corrupt governments still tacitly allow it to flourish, despite it having been outlawed by numerous international treaties. Bales explains, "This is an economic crime. People do not enslave people to be mean to them; they do it to make a profit."

Human trafficking in numbers

- *50% of trafficking victims were trafficked into sexual exploitation and 38% for forced labour*

- *67% of people trafficked for sexual exploitation are women*

- *67% of people investigated or arrested for trafficking in persons are men, and 33% women*

- *46% of trafficking victims are women, 34% are children, and 20% are men*

*(Estimates by The United Nations Office for Drugs and Crime (2020) UNODC.*The Church of England had links to slavery through United Society for the Propagation of the Gospel (USPG) missionary organisations, which had plantations in Barbados.

The bishop of Exeter personally owned slaves.

The British government paid out millions – the equivalent of around 17 billion pounds today – to compensate slave owners for the lost capital associated with freeing slaves. This payout was a massive 40% of the government's budget and required many bonds to slave owners to effectuate the law. It is estimated that one sixth of the countries estates were bought with the money from the Government handouts to slave owner families.

The pay-outs went to 47,000 individuals and families. These ranged from high ranking aristocrats running large sugar plantations to lowly widows who kept a few slaves as passive income.

THREE PROMINENT BENEFICIARIES

JOHN GLADSTONE – £106,769.

The equivalent of £12 million ($15.59 million) in government payments today.

His son William Gladstone went on to be Prime Minister of Great Britain four times between 1868 and 1894. The family still owns a very large estate in Wales.

WILLIAM JOLLIFFE – £4,000

Who had 164 slaves.

JOHN SAWBRIDGE ERLE-DRAX – £4,293

He owned a plantation in Barbados still in operation today. He received his compensation for 189 slaves that worked on the Drax Hall plantation.

John's latest descendant, is now the Member of Parliament for South Dorset. He is also the biggest private landowner in Dorset, controlling more than 15,000 acres of the county.

AFTER THOUGHTS

The slavery of Gypsies is as I have shown is entrenched within history. From the very earliest times right through to modern times of the present age. Gypsy Roma Travellers have endured barbarism from all nations and within all civilisations throughout history. They were taken as slaves by invading armies in wars, taken by pirates at sea and on land often by privateers under commission. They were imprisoned for vagrancy, transported to far off lands, used as galley slaves, used to work the sugar and tobacco plantations on colonies in the new world and in recent times deprived of their heritage their right to roam through unjust laws. Gypsies were sold on blocks in the common markets of the East as well as Caribbean island of Barbados and the sea ports of England and France. The established church denounced them as heathens and ungodly whist numerous kings and queens brought in numerous Acts throughout the centuries to rid their countries of these vagrants. Many were hung or sentenced to a life of slavery or imprisonment. They were hunted, tortured chained and victimised by every nation including the Cromwell and Nazi regimes.

SORROWS

For all those years of tragedy and pain
I suffer not to have thee back again
though prejudice will soar its ugly head
though I suffer fools gladly lest pretend
their gracious words I comprehend

Through years of suffering of the cross
I bear no foolish rhetoric at a loss
I count my blessings awhile each day
amongst my foolish prayers
and whilst aware

of hurts and painful whips and more
that stroke upon my body soiled and sore

And yet I bear no feelings of remorse
my travels on this ship of life
im well rehearsed
for sorrow holds no bitter sweet comfort to be
only the hope of grace so yet to see
Oh Lord give me the strength to endure this loss of liberty

So that at the end of passions I can declare
I took the world she offered
the only love of me
yet desperate and broke
I awoke to sorrows
oh foolish me

Ray Wills

SOURCES AND RESOURCES

The Pariah Syndrome: An Account of Gypsy Slavery and Persecution IAN HANCOCK

A history of the Gypsies – Walter Simson

The Gypsies- Charles Leland 1882

Gypsies a persecuted race – William A Duna 1985

The Gypsies in the Byzantine Empire and the Balkans in the late middle ages – George Soulis published by Archivarius

The world their homeland-Francois de Foletier

Le folklore de lesbos Georgeakis and Leon Pineau

History and Politics From India to Europe Byzantium

ROMBASE By Milena Alincova May Prague Czech Republic

Myths, Hypotheses and facts concerning the origin of peoples The true origin of Roma and Sinti -Avraham Sandor- Hutchinson Robert Davis

- Christian Slaves, Muslim Masters: White Slavery In The Mediterranean, The Barbary Coast, And Italy, 1500-1800 (Palgrave Macmillan).

Books by M Paul Batillard -
BELZEC, SOBIBOR, TREBLINKA – the Operation Reinhard Death Camps Indiana University Press – Yitzhak Arad, 1987. ISBN 0-253-3429-7

Paul Baepler -White Slaves, African Masters: An Anthology of American Barbary Captivity Narratives

Friedman, Philip.- The Extermination of the Gypsie
TIMES GONE

Gypsies and Travellers – Robert Dawson

John Oldmixon,-The British Empire in America, vol. 2,

Hoffman-They Were White and They Were Slaves

Matthew Parker- The Sugar Barons WINDMILL BOOKS 2012

History of Barbados - Sir Richard Schomburg (2012),

Bishop Gilbert Burnet- History of His Own Time

A CONCISE HISTORY OF BARBADOS- JOHN MOORE

https//blackhistory neocities.org/Barbados_History. html

To Hell or Barbadus

  - Sean Ocallaghan -Brandon 2000

Bill of Sale of GYPSY SLAVES IN MOLDAVIA 1851 – Dr M.
Gaster - GYPSY LORE JOURNAL

Dalby Thomas - An Historical Account of the Rise and Growth of
the British West Indies.

The History of Barbados- Sir Richard Schomburg

BARBADOS - A TRUE AND EXACT HISTORY RICHARD
LIGON- HACKETT PUBLISHING 2011

THE TIME TRAVELLER- RAY WILLS AMAZON 2022

John Oldmixon --The British Empire in America.

DUNN R S -Sugar and Slaves LONDON 1973

ELLIS A.B – White Slaves and Bondservants in the plantations Argosy Georgetown British Guinea 1883

PUCKREIN G.A – Little England plantation Society and Anglo Barbadian politics 1627-1700 NEW YORK 1984

ERIC WILLIAMS From Columbus to Castro A History of the Carabbean 1492-1969 LONDON 1972

Simon Webb – The forgotten SLAVE TRADE

BRITISH GYPSY SLAVERY-The Caribbean and America-ROBERT DAWSON Blackwell Derbyshire

THE FORGOTTEN TRADE   NIGEL TATTERSFIELD 1991.

ETHNIC MINORITIES LYME REGIS & WEST DORSET PAST AND PRESENT

LOUISA PARKER, JUDY FORD and JO DRAPER

LYME REGIS MUSEUM 2004

EMPIRES OF THE SEA

 ROGER CROWLEY - FABER AND FABER 2008

WHITE SLAVERY IN THE BARBARY STATES

CHARLES SUMNER ENHANCED MEDIA 2017

GYPSY FOLK TALES

FRANCIS HINDES GROOME

UNIVERSITY PRESS OF THE PACIFIC 2002

Ruth Mazo Karras SLAVERY AND SOCIETY IN MEDIEVAL SCANDINAVIA"

WHITE SLAVERY IN BARBARY STATES - CHARLES SUMMER

THE IRISH SLAVES - RHETTA AKAMATSU

SUGAR IN THE BLOOD – ANDREA STUART
PORTOBELLA BOOKS 2012H

WHITE GOLD – GILES MILTON

Hodder and Stoughton 2004

SLAVERY – JEREMY BLACK

Robinson 2011

PIRATES OF BARBARY – ADRIAN TINNISWOOD
Vintage Books 2011

The PROJECT GUTNBURG ebook - The Story of the Barbary Corsairs, by Stanley Lane-Poole.

THE SLAVE TRADE- HUGH THOMAS
Papermac 1998.

Printed in Great Britain
by Amazon

21427421R00119